Managing *for* Quality

How to Implement and Manage a Business Strategy of Continuous Improvement

Leslie L. Kossoff

Kossoff Management Consulting
Burlingame, California

Managing for Quality: How to Implement and Manage a Business Strategy of Continuous Improvement by Leslie L. Kossoff
© 1998 by Leslie L. Kossoff

Formerly *Closing the Gap: The Handbook for Total Quality Implementation*
First Edition © 1992 by Leslie L. Kossoff
Second Edition © 1994 by Leslie L. Kossoff

Kossoff Management Consulting
1534 Plaza Lane, No. 356
Burlingame, California 94010
tel: 650 697 8440
fax: 650 697 8990
www.kossoff.com

Cover Design: Dunn+Associates
Interior Design: Sara Patton Book Production Services
Back Cover: Susan Kendrick Writing
Photo: Mark Jordan

Printed in the United States of America
Library of Congress Catalog Card Number: 98-65723
ISBN 0-9630724-3-9

To J. B. F.

Contents

Acknowledgments

By the time a book reaches its third edition, as has this one, the list of those to whom appreciation is due is extensive. It is also also assured that there will be some people missing. To those, I extend my thanks as well as my apologies for the oversight.

I have had the great benefit of both learning and support throughout the journey of this book. In particular, my appreciation is extended to my clients and students, from whom I have learned so much.

The insight and comments received have been both appreciated and reflected as the book has evolved. My thanks go to Don Antenore, Craig Hagopian, Dr. Harriet Kandelman, Wayne Kimball, Lee Rizio, Ken Romans, and Tony Wainwright, among others. Particular appreciation is extended to my great friend and colleague, Dr. Marlene Coleman as well as to Dottie Walters, mentor and friend, for their support as well as for reminding me of the ongoing importance of the field.

My appreciation is also extended to Bruce Beatty. He, through his teaching and without either of our knowledge, provided me with my first interest in, insight into, and understanding of the field improvement.

My everlasting gratitude is extended to Dr. W. Edwards Deming. Even though years have passed since his death, his teachings, guidance, and belief in me still act as touchstones.

Thanks also go to my design team for their creativity and support. The talent and patience exhibited by Kathi Dunn, Susan Kendrick, and Sara Patton are greatly appreciated.

Finally, as in all things, family and friends played a part in this as with any effort of merit. My thanks go to George Conley, friend and teacher, my brother, David, for demonstrating so clearly that change and commitment to change can be a gift, and, most particularly, to Jose Fernandez, because of whom, in so many ways, this book has been possible.

Preface

A lovely aspect of the passage of time is that one gets to find out how things turn out.

When the first edition of this book was published in 1992, Quality was the most popular buzz of its day. Total Quality was the bandwagon onto which organizations were hopping, and everyone was trying to establish themselves as an active part of the Quality Movement. Gurus abounded and theories collided.

It was both an active and a trying time for industry.

At that time the purpose of the book was to provide a calm in the storm of activity. *Closing the Gap* between theory and application (the basis for its original title) was its purpose. The book was, and is, designed to provide Managers with the knowledge and structure to be able to move Quality away from being a "want to have" and into being "the way we do business."

Over the course of time Quality has become an expectation in and for organizations. Products and services are differentiated and purchases decided upon based on the levels of Quality which are provided. While Quality has not yet become a standardized way of doing business, it has become an integrated part of the customers' expectations and, as such, of the Manager's responsibilities.

Customers and consumers now discriminate based on Quality. And they can. Enough organizations have shown that levels of Quality which meet and exceed that which has been done before can be and are the norms. This has created a level of performance pressure for organizations far exceeding any time in the past.

It is no longer acceptable or viable to simply turn out a product or service. Whether internal or external to the organization, discriminating consumers will find alternatives if the product or service being provided does not meet their needs.

What does this mean for the Manager?

It's simple. Find out what constitutes Quality for your part of and for the whole of the organization, find out what is keeping you from getting there—and staying there—and do something about it.

Find out who your customers are both internal and external to the organization. You may be surprised at the extent and diversity of that definition. Find out how they use whatever it is you supply. And find out who else they are using as suppliers both in direct competition with you and for other goods and services altogether. That will provide a base level needs and expectations assessment.

Make sure you understand why you and your people do what you do within the organization. And make sure your people understand the impact of their actions on the larger organization and its purpose.

No matter at what level, use Quality as your Business Strategy.

Quality is not an intangible or amorphous commodity. In fact, it is the strategic and tactical basis for any decision which should or needs to be made.

How will this action or direction affect what we do? What is the impact internally? Externally? For our customers? On our competitors? What can and must we learn from our customers and competitors in order to stay in and, preferably, grow our market?

Strategic Quality is highly defined and tactically manifest. It is an active thinking and doing process involving all people associated with the organization. Everyone is involved. No one is exempt.

While many years have passed and the buzz of Quality has lifted, the need for Quality is greater than ever before. Joseph Juran said that while the Twentieth Century was the Century of Technology, the Twenty-First Century will be the Century of Quality.

I believe that he is correct. Businesses can no longer differentiate themselves by product or service alone. Borders, within and outside of organizations as well as countries, no longer exist as we have known them. Anyone can get access to most anything in ways never dreamed of before. And that puts the pressure on the organization to be the organization of choice.

To do that, every Manager at every level must actively work as an integrated whole, in concert with the direction and vision of the Executive Team, to create the Quality that ensures that everything that they and their people do works towards the organization's goals. Nothing less will succeed.

PART 1

Introduction & Overview

CHAPTER 1

Why Quality?

Goals and Objectives

There is a certain romance in the idea of pursuing all that is right and good. That notion is never more apparent than in an organization actively pursuing Quality.

Each of us, as we begin our foray into Quality implementation, actually begins a quest. As we continue on our journey, we will create and realize an organizational life which is based on the objectives of the organization in meeting and exceeding the customers' needs. We will be establishing an environment which is based on a win-win philosophy.

No one is ever a loser in a Quality organization. But how do we get there? And for what are we searching?

The Quest

Each person in every organization involved in Quality implementation is on a quest for Total Customer Satisfaction.

This means that the customer and his needs are paramount in everything done in the organization. This quest never ends. Once begun, no matter what we accomplish, we must always be looking for ways to improve upon our past.

There is no such thing as resting on laurels in a Quality organization. Frankly, there isn't time. No sooner will an organization establish a new market, or regain competitive position in an old one, but one of their competitors follows suit with some other innovation. Customers have the right to be selective—and they exercise that right at will.

To succeed in the quest, the initial focus must be on **Quality** in every aspect of everything we do. The concept of Quality must be first and foremost in our minds as we work. We must look for situations in which Quality is not being implemented and find ways to improve. We must also look at ways in which Quality is apparent in what we do and build from there.

Understanding relates to our customers' needs. This means both internal and external customers. Each person in the organization must know his customer, his needs, and then focus on how to not only meet—but exceed—those needs.

Simply satisfying the customer is not enough. Customers must be delighted with everything we do.

Next, like Quality, **excellence** must be a focal point in all activities. Organizations can only remain viable if they truly *excel* in their market area.

Every market is extremely competitive. The only way to ensure marketshare is by being the organization which customers believe they can trust because of the consistency and excellence of products and services.

Service is a watchword across all industries. It is also one which is commonly misunderstood. The tendency among manufacturing organizations is to think that service is not a primary motivation in Quality. And many service organizations think that they already have all the service-related Quality requirements.

In fact, neither is correct. Both manufacturing and service industries must look at the service requirements of their customers—both internal and external.

What are the service criteria? Are there any standards which either already have been or should be established? Typical service criteria include timeliness, accuracy, and cost. Any organization can look at both its internal and external requirements and apply those criteria to its performance.

Lastly, **technology** must be considered as it applies to customer satisfaction. This applies as much to existing technology as to developing technologies.

Each person should identify the types of technologies used to support the process. Are those technologies being used to their greatest effect? Are there ways we can use the existing technology to improve customer perceptions of our products and services? How can we improve upon that technology?

Combining the factors of Quality, Understanding, Excellence, Service, and Technology into a coordinated and cohesive effort will give both internal and external customers the satisfaction they both desire—and deserve. It will also ensure continuing existence in a marketplace which must contend with constantly increasing competition.

Defining Quality

The challenge in defining Quality is that it manifests itself differently in each organization. In fact, from department to department and from division to division of the same organization, Quality will look slightly different.

And this is only right. The only way for Quality to be successfully implemented is to avoid "cookbook" approaches.

No one, no matter who they might be, can tell you that because a particular implementation method worked in a comparable organization—or even another part of the same organization—that it will work anyplace else.

Quality is the ultimate customized effort. While the basic objectives and principles are the same, each organization will implement it differently.

Still, it's only fair that Quality gets some form of definition. And so ...

Quality is the unrelenting pursuit of continuous improvement throughout an organization which is realized by accessing and utilizing the concerted knowledge and experience of managers and employees at all levels in a data-driven, cooperative, coordinated, and systematic approach.

As you can see from the definition, the Quality process, once begun, has no finish line. That is why Quality is not just another program but a business strategy which permeates all aspects of the organization. Continuous improvement means that "perfection" is not static. What we want to call "perfection" can still be improved upon.

An integral part of the Quality process is the utilization of knowledge and expertise of people in the organization. People are, by far, the most untapped resource in the organization.

While we think about capital investment or designing new information systems to improve an operation, rarely do we think of asking the people who work the processes day-in and day-out how they would recommend it be improved. It becomes clear in a very short time that this untapped resource has a higher return than any investment ever made.

You will also note that the definition specifies Managers be included in the process. This, again, is an often overlooked aspect of the Quality process.

There is a common misconception that Quality, flattening the organization, and laying off middle managers are the same thing. This is not the case.

Managers have a world of knowledge and expertise, not only about the areas they manage but also about the management process itself. It is in the best interests of the organization to access the knowledge and the ability of all levels of Management to fully realize a Quality success.

A data-driven approach is necessary in a Quality environment. Historically, too many decisions have been made based on someone's thoughts or feelings. As a result, we have spent a lot of time working on symptoms, often entirely missing the root cause.

Instead, in a Quality organization, data are used to identify real issues, get at their root causes, and develop corrective actions. Then, the pilot implementation of the corrective action is measured to determine whether the change is affecting the problem in the desired direction. *In a Quality organization, it is said, there are no opinions. Only data.*

A cooperative effort is required as it does no good whatsoever if a change which is made in one area adversely effects another area. It is imperative that information flow throughout the organization so that teams and Management know what the other areas are doing, and add their expertise wherever it is needed.

This leads to the coordination of the Quality effort. It is an all too common mistake in organizations just beginning the

Quality process to take a shot-gun approach to implementation.

The tendency is to want everyone involved as quickly as possible. Whether it is participating in training, forming teams, or implementing corrective action activities, many organizations mandate one hundred percent participation from the first. This is an unrealistic and counter-strategic way of addressing the process.

Instead of insisting on everyone's involvement at the very first, it makes much better sense to phase the implementation to address the needs and the strategies of the organization. Management must coordinate the efforts to ensure that there is no duplication or contradiction of effort.

Remember that Quality is a business strategy—not simply an improvement program. And as such, implementation decisions should match the overall strategy of the organization.

It is recommended that people not involved in immediate efforts be kept apprised of team activities. It is also recommended that every member of the organization—no matter at what level—understand from the first that no one is exempt from the Quality process. Everyone will participate—which is why Quality is a systematic approach to the organization.

Management as well as team systems must be developed to support the Quality effort. Activities and responsibilities must be leveraged to include time for team activities. In fact, no one should be faced with the added responsibility of team activity without first having their Management review their activities with them, determining which does not add value, and can thus be set aside.

We would all like to believe that everything we do adds value. Yet, the estimates of actual time spent on any product or service which adds value ranges from one-half of one to five percent. Thus, the initial obstacle of "I don't have the time" is most likely one which can be set aside relatively quickly.

Another aspect of building a Quality system is that of corrective action response. There is nothing more frustrating than for a team to work devotedly—identifying improvement opportunities, developing the data collection system, and designing a corrective action recommendation—only to receive no response from immediate or upper Management once the recommendation has been submitted.

Management must be prepared from the first to respond to recommendations immediately. If not, the team members will rightfully distrust Management's commitment to Quality and the effort will die before it has really begun.

By being unrelenting in your pursuit of continuous improvement, you ensure delighted customers. At the same time you are reducing operating costs and increasing profits. Everyone wins.

Quality is Not ...

Having spent so much time on what Quality is, it is only fair to define what Quality is not. Unfortunately, there are many more examples of the latter than the former.

First of all, Quality is not another "quick fix" program. There is nothing at all quick about Quality. Yes, the organization realizes gains in a relatively short time period. That comes from the coordinated team approach that is necessary in the implementation process. But to establish a true Quality organization takes time and attention and relentless commitment to the process.

Second, Quality is not a religion. There is no "conversion" to Quality. And there are no miracles. Quality takes a lot of study, analysis, work, and more work. Once begun, it can never be forgotten because it is apparent in every area of the organization.

Managers and employees, alike, hold each other responsible for behaviors being congruent with the Quality philosophy. And, while the theorists may be referred to as "gurus," they are not. They are, however, learned people who have developed theories which are being implemented as "Quality"—no more no less.

Quality is a business strategy. It is a hard-line, money-oriented approach to business—and also happens to be the most humane business operating approach to have come along in the twentieth century.

Third, Quality is neither parades nor banners. It is not fancy slogans and posters plastered all over the walls. In fact, the more insidious the process the less chance there is for people who would normally balk to do so.

An excellent strategy is to form a team with a specific strategic issue in mind, allow the team members to work the improvement process, and then, when they finish, tell them that they have just participated in a Quality effort.

Finally, Quality is neither teams nor measurement techniques. It should not be confused with the tools which support it.

Quality is a holistic approach to improvement of all aspects of the organization. It is a redefinition of the purpose and direction of the organization. And it is the *only* hope organizations have for ongoing success.

Objectives of Quality

There are three main objectives to the Quality initiative. Each is definable and measurable. And each will be manifest in different ways by different organizations. Nonetheless, the objectives remain the same. They are:

- Reduction of variation in all aspects of the operation

- Building systems for continuous improvement

- Optimization of all aspects of the organization

  - Building on the best.

  - Reduction of waste.

  - Cooperation and coordination between all departments, divisions, and organizations.

Reduction of Variation in All Aspects of the Operation

It is important to remember that while the manifestation of Quality is through management systems and team participation, the roots of Quality come from statistics.

The way to create and maintain Quality is through consistent reduction of variation. Variation, quite simply, consists of those things within the organization which change. The question is, where are those changes coming from and are they in the best interests of the organization?

Variation occurs as a result of decisions made, unfortunately, most often by Management. Variation can occur as a result of loosely defined specifications or requirements, multiple suppliers, or a poorly trained workforce.

Decisions which result in a reduction of variation come from an understanding of how the variation got in in the first place. Are the job requirements clearly defined? Do people know how to do their jobs? Are suppliers brought in to the process so that they understand how the product or service they provide impacts the organization?

From the start it is important to learn how to use meaningful statistics towards identifying what variation exists, where it is coming from, and whether it is acceptable to the organization.

- By focusing on the reduction of variation, arbitrary measures become meaningless.

- Instead of working to specifications, we should be working to optimal levels of operation.

- Instead of using subjective appraisal systems, we should be managing processes and employees in a consistent, supportive, and participative manner.

In other words, whether it is product, service, or personnel, we must identify where variation in the system exists, determine the cause of the variation, and identify means of reducing it.

Building Systems for Continuous Improvement

Quality doesn't happen by accident. A systemic approach to Quality ensures buy-in at all levels. It also allows the organization to avoid many common obstacles and pitfalls encountered during the implementation process.

For example, in order to successfully build a Quality organization, it is first necessary to develop systems for continuous improvement.

This means that Management must begin by establishing a vision for the organization. Once that vision has been developed, it must be shared and discussed with the next level of Management.

As the process progresses, each level of Management has the opportunity to ask questions and to challenge the information presented. Tactical implementation issues can be discussed and next steps identified. At each step along the way, the next level becomes the champion who will present the information and support its implementation.

Systems of continuous improvement build responsibility and accountability into the Quality system.

Optimization of All Aspects of the Organization

To optimize an organization is to create the most favorable conditions possible within that entity. Thus, by optimizing all aspects of the organization, we build systems to ensure the establishment and maintenance of those favorable conditions. This objective is manifest in three ways.

■ It begins with *building on the best.*

A common misconception which creates a large number of problems is that Quality means dropping everything that has been done before as if it had no value. This is both incorrect and insulting. Quality is based on the premise that you first build on the best. Then, you work to improve whatever needs to be improved.

By saying that nothing done before has any value, we are directly attacking the people who worked hard to develop what they considered to be improved ways of doing business. In fact, those changes may have made perfect sense when developed, but have lost their value over time.

We must focus on what *does* work in order to identify what doesn't. We can also use the best of the organization to study and learn why those systems, processes, or techniques worked. That information can then be used as a basis for improvement in other aspects of the organization.

■ The second manifestation of optimization is to *reduce waste.*

Improvement opportunities are most apparent where waste can be detected. And waste is not just defined by dollars lost or materials scrapped. Waste is also defined in terms of time, energy, and effort.

Each person in the organization must look at his process to identify where value is added and where it is not. He must then look beyond to determine what is being wasted at that point of the process.

These are the opportunities for improvement which will net the greatest return to both the individual and the organization. From the individual's perspective, they are no longer faced with the prospect of wasted time and energy. This results in greater satisfaction with the workplace and the job at hand. From the organization's perspective, the time and materials wasted can be replaced with value-added activities. Cycle time will be reduced and operating costs will lessen.

■ Finally, unless there is *cooperation and coordination between all departments, divisions, and organizations,* there is an extremely high risk that the Quality effort will not succeed.

It is imperative that everyone in the Management ranks understand and agree upon the strategy and direction of the organization. They must then be able to communicate that information to the people who report to them.

As the Quality initiative progresses, it is incumbent upon Management to monitor activities to ensure that all team activities are pointed in the same direction. There is no excuse for allowing a team to pursue an improvement opportunity if it is in conflict with the organization's goals or if Management has no intention of implementing the corrective action recommended.

Teams should be so conversant with the organization's goals and direction that they can justify the ways by which their suggested improvement will support the organization's strategic goals. And Management should be able to identify any peripheral or tangential activities on the part of a team so that they can be brought back into line.

In a more mature Quality environment, managers and employees challenge each other to explain how a questionable activity supports the overall strategy of the organization. This demonstrates shared goals as well as increased trust between levels of the operation.

Management must ensure every employee understands the logic behind Quality—its intent, definition, and objectives. Only by doing this can the organization be assured that once the Quality effort begins, everyone is working in the same direction with the same ultimate goal in mind.

CHAPTER 2

Principles of Quality

While each of the theories about Quality differ to a degree, there are some consistent principles which must be understood and implemented in order to ensure success. These principles apply just as much to Management as to the employees.

The important thing is that there be consistency in their implementation and in the approach to that implementation across the organization. Managers and employees, alike, should be assured that they will be working with the same rules and expectations—no matter to which part of the organization they belong.

There are twelve fundamental principles which will be discussed. They are:

- Focus on the Customer
- Constancy of Purpose
- Supplier Involvement
- Management Leadership and Commitment
- Continuous Improvement
- Reduction of Waste
- Structured Problem Solving and Data
- Planning for Quality

- Continuous Learning
- Cooperation and Coordination
- Importance of People and Teamwork
- Pride and Dignity

Each of these is an intrinsic part of the Quality philosophy. Together, they allow us to succeed in our ability to fulfill the goals of continuous improvement toward customer satisfaction. Let's consider each one individually.

Focus on the Customer

Yes, you've heard this before. However, it cannot be stressed strongly enough. Only by keeping an eye on customer needs and goals can we ensure that we are utilizing our time and our effort in the most valuable way.

If we focus on individual or internal goals and intentions —without checking them against those of the customer—we can conceivably come up with some wonderful and innovative ideas. If there is no market, however, we've wasted our time.

And those who are at mid-point in the process must not only consider the immediate customer, but also think about the ultimate customer.

We often unintentionally limit ourselves by giving credence only to our immediate external customer. But if that customer provides the product to a consumer, then whose needs are we really trying to meet and exceed?

While we must work closely with distributors of products or services, we must clearly focus on those by whom the product or service will be used. After all, if we produce a high Quality product, at a fair market price, which is delivered to

18

our distributors in a timely manner—but that no one wants to buy—what good is it to anyone?

Now let's extend the focus to the internal customer for a moment. A very common human tendency is to get so locked into our own responsibilities that we forget that whatever we produce as our end-product or output, then becomes the input that the next person will be using to begin his process. If we focus on the needs of the internal customers, we greatly reduce the chance that we will have wasted our time and theirs by providing a useless product which, while it completes our task assignment, does no good whatsoever.

Think about it. Is there anything more frustrating than being the next step in the process and knowing that whatever is received from the previous step, your first action will be to rework it in some way? It is well worth the time and effort to talk between internal customers and suppliers to ensure that no one's time at any step of the process is being wasted.

Constancy of Purpose

While this principle applies to all levels of the organization, the primary focus must be in Management. It is only possible to succeed in implementing Quality if Management is unrelenting in their attention to the principles and actions involved. This principle is the one which employees will be waiting for Management to violate—and with good reason.

If we think about the programs that have been implemented in the past, we see that each has ostensibly been different— because each was going to be the "new way of doing business." Each time, we see that Management, at some point, changed its mind. And every time that happened, employees were once again left with the feeling that all their attention and work on the "new way" was for naught.

In a Quality environment, Management must take the lead by creating a system in which employees *can* implement continuous improvement. More importantly, Management must demonstrate their own commitment and constancy of purpose by visibly implementing continuous improvement on their own processes.

Another means of demonstrating constancy of purpose is to avoid the "cherry-picking" that we so often see among the principles of Quality. Develop a plan and stick with it. With Quality, either you are doing it or you are not. There is no in-between.

Employees must also assist in establishing and maintaining constancy of purpose throughout the organization. When provided with training to learn new skills, use them. Look at your processes in a different way than before. Be innovative. Use all of your skills to assist the organization in accomplishing all that it can.

Constancy of Purpose is a principle which reminds us that we have begun this process, it is never ending, and we must remain committed to it.

Supplier Involvement

This principle is another which has both internal and external ramifications.

If you, as an internal customer, are having difficulty with the product which you receive from the previous process step, make the effort to involve your suppliers in your process. Ask them to discuss with you how their output is used. Explain your process to them. Describe your concerns. Allow them to become involved in creating solutions.

This also applies to external suppliers. It's easy for us to simply place blame elsewhere—only it doesn't accomplish anything. Instead of placing blame, contact your supplier and discuss ways and means of improving your relationship.

The premise that suppliers want to keep us as customers is one which stands well-grounded in logic. As long as we remain in business and have need for their services, the more opportunity for the supplier, too, to survive and thrive. Therefore, it is also in the supplier's best interest to be involved in ways which demonstrate their value.

Many organizations maintain high numbers of suppliers for the same part or service. Logic would dictate that the more suppliers, the safer the organization in case of emergency.

Based on the premise that variation must be reduced in order to ensure Quality, the logic of multiple suppliers doesn't always hold. Yes, the organization may be able to access a large number of parts or immediate service in a short amount of time. But if that product or service is unusable or markedly different from others being used, what good is it?

Rather than building an outsize number of suppliers, the organization is better advised to work with a smaller number of suppliers who understand its needs. Develop cooperative relationships with suppliers. But, be aware. It is unfair to dump your problems into the supplier's lap simply because you don't want to take responsibility for your own actions.

Before you contact any supplier—internal or external— make sure you have at least a basic understanding of your own process. Create a process flow diagram which you can study to determine how your process is being effected by the suppliers. Share that diagram with them so that they can better understand your process and become knowledgeable enough to make recommendations for improvement.

Work together to make things work.

Management Leadership and Commitment

The role of Management is one which changes drastically during the Quality effort. Historically we've been used to using Management time to oversee day-to-day operations.

When you think about it, this is one of the most apparent wastes in an organization. Promotions to Management positions are rarely made because a person seems like a good choice to oversee day-to-day operations. Instead, decisions to promote are based just as much on a person's content knowledge as on his ability to listen, learn, lead others, and innovate. Then what do we do once they've been promoted? Never give them the opportunity to do any of those things!

In a Quality environment, managers at all levels are given the opportunity to bring out the best in themselves as well as in their employees. One of the ways by which they can do so is to demonstrate their leadership—rather than just management—of the organization.

Management is responsible for demonstrating its own efforts to implement the Quality philosophy. Managers are responsible for working consistently and continuously to create an environment which allows both themselves and their employees to fully implement Quality.

Managers must focus on their own processes in order to determine opportunities for improvement. They must also use their knowledge of the organization and the processes they manage to assist in the development of long-term visions for the organization.

While we tend to look at Quality as untapping only the employee resource, we should also look at the possibilities it opens for the Management group.

Reciprocally, employees have to help. The only way that Management can satisfactorily demonstrate its support is if employees communicate their needs—whatever they are—to Management.

One of the most interesting outcomes of a Quality environment is that it soon becomes clear that the employees are the customers and Management the suppliers.

Management demonstrates its leadership abilities and commitment to the Quality process by clearing obstacles out of the way of the employees' improvement efforts. Management also creates a risk-supporting environment which lends itself to innovation.

But what are the obstacles? And where do the risks lie? These questions can only be satisfactorily answered by employees. And unless the employees believe that they are not taking a high risk by informing their Management of those obstacles and risks, improvement and innovation will be stifled from the first.

And so, we are back to leadership and commitment. Managers must learn to act as suppliers to their employees. They must work to determine their needs and to identify obstacles to their success. And employees must be treated as customers —by learning what it will take not only to meet, but to exceed their needs.

Continuous Improvement

If there is a watchword for the Quality effort, it is "continuous improvement." We must constantly strive to improve everything we do. Nothing and no one is exempt from improvement.

This concept must be constantly on everyone's minds—at all times. No matter what it is you are working on you must look for ways to improve it.

Each person must feel a sense of responsibility for improvement to the product or service or system. Break away from the idea that because something has always been done a particular way, that is the only way that it can or should be done.

There is no finish line in Quality—a concept based on the idea of continuous improvement. If we are continuously improving everything we do, there is no such thing as perfection. Only better and better and better.

Be strategic about improvement. Look for opportunities which need to be addressed first. And then, once an improvement has been implemented, make sure it sticks and then move on to another.

Franklin Delano Roosevelt said,

> *"Do something.*
> *If it works, do more of it.*
> *If it doesn't work, do something else."*

24

Use continuous improvement as a way to allow yourself to expand and create and have fun.

Reduction of Waste

Historically, the tendency has been to categorize waste as material items with dollar value. As we have progressed, we have learned that waste refers just as much to time and energy as it does to materials. Just because we can dollarize an item doesn't mean that it is the only thing that can be wasted.

One of the most frustrating things anyone can face is having worked on a project of some kind, and then being told that their work wasn't needed. This also applies when you have been given inadequate instructions, you move forward with the information at hand, and subsequently find out that what you've produced isn't what was being looked for. That feeling of frustration is so all-inclusive that it extends to other assignments and activities which have nothing to do with the wasted effort.

The most apparent improvement opportunities can be identified by looking for waste in the process. Identify activities which don't seem to add any value to the product or service on which you are working. Chances are there is wasted time or materials at that point. Work with your customers and suppliers to determine what needs exist for the product or service. Identify opportunities to streamline your efforts while at the same time ensuring the Quality and usefulness of your product or service at each point of the process.

On the employee level, if there are questions about why you are performing an activity, ask your immediate manager. Keep in mind that it is just as important for employees to know *why* they are doing their jobs as it is for them to know *how* to do it.

It may be that a process activity should be changed so that it will make sense. Or, if there is no real justification for that activity, it can be abandoned. And if you see what you think is waste occurring at another point in the process, address it. If it is not within your span of responsibility or control, talk to the person who is responsible.

Be unrelenting. Don't let anything get by.

Structured Problem Solving and Data

This principle is one which absolutely cannot be violated in a Quality environment. The only way to determine whether a change is an improvement—or simply a tampering with the system—is through structured problem solving which uses data.

You will recall that one of the basic objectives of a Quality effort is to reduce variation in all aspects of the operation. The only way by which that can be accomplished—and the only way by which we know that the changes we are making will optimize the organization—is through data.

Still, many people at all levels are concerned about the data aspects of Quality. This is where we have an opportunity to learn from our mistakes.

First of all, we have finally learned that we gain nothing by measuring everything to death. Data collection and reporting are *strategic*. Measurement systems must be designed and developed according to the goals of the organization. Critical measurement points should be identified. Only those critical points should have any measurement system attached to them.

Some people are concerned about the difficulty of collecting and reporting data. Rest assured that for the vast majority involved in this pursuit, higher math is not required. For the most part, the measurements only require basic math skills. The rigors of advanced mathematics and statistics are reserved for the people who enjoy applying those techniques.

And, finally, for those of you who believe that what you do simply cannot be measured: you're wrong. Keep in mind that when it comes to data, qualitative is just as important as quantitative. Measurement of your process may simply require a process flow diagram and cause-effect analysis. These data can provide rich guidance towards the identification and solution of problems within a process.

Remember that measurement is really only a part of the overall Quality effort. It plays an important role—but only because we want to make the best decisions possible.

Planning for Quality

Everything you do must first be planned and thought out with an eye towards Quality. This isn't only for new products but also for existing day-to-day activities.

Take a few moments before you begin on a new activity and think about how you can build in and plan for Quality as part of your performance. Determine the obstacles which keep you from being able to successfully complete that activity. Those obstacles are your opportunities to reduce waste and continuously improve your process.

Identify potential data sources which will help you determine corrective actions. If none exist, begin planning for the measurement systems which will provide you with those data.

Be proactive. Don't allow the existing process or system to keep you from expanding your thinking about how to find a better way.

Planning for Quality may seemingly slow down a process or system at first. However, the thought and problem-solving that occurs before a task begins will save the employee and the organization vast amounts of time during process performance. Further, the need for correction and rework will be reduced. Ultimately, this will result in direct cost savings and avoidances for the organization.

Continuous Learning

A Quality effort requires a great deal of training. More importantly, however, to fully succeed each person in every aspect of the operation must be dedicated to the principle of continuous learning.

One of the commitments of a Quality organization is the study and analysis of every system and process existing within the organization's bounds. Ultimately, that task extends to the analysis of how the systems and processes of customers and suppliers affect the internal bounds of the organization. In order to understand the relationships and inter-relationships of those systems and processes, we must be prepared to take adequate time to study.

It is no longer acceptable to give a cursory look and make decisions. All decisions must be coordinated with those who would be effected. We must be prepared to exert ourselves to learn more about our systems and processes than we ever thought possible—or necessary.

In some cases, resources for learning will have to be accessed from outside the organization. Many employees and managers will find themselves wanting to go back to school to access specialized learning. But for many, the learning will be a dedicated effort inside the organization.

Quality cannot be rushed. It took many years to establish the ways we do business now. It will also take time to first, understand what needs to be changed, and then, using appropriate data, make those changes.

Cooperation and Coordination

The concept of optimization is one which is based, in large part, on systems of cooperation and coordination. When we learn what it takes to improve the operation, we are then dependent upon our ability to coordinate efforts to ensure success.

Previously, team activities in organizations have focused only on the immediate activities of the individual groups. This has resulted in some excellent recommendations, but very little implementation or ongoing success. By focusing on cooperation and coordination from the first, negative internal competition is lessened. People all know that they are working for the greater good.

Cooperative systems also allow an easier transition to cross-functionality. By gathering groups of people from different functions, but who are all working towards the same goal, the chances for success are increased exponentially. After all, the obstacles which would usually be creating havoc later are identified and dealt with at the beginning of the process.

By letting everyone in the organization know the goals and direction of the operation, team efforts can be coordinated and phased strategically. This will create an improved information flow and faster decision making.

The onus for the cooperative system initially rests exclusively in Management hands. It is incumbent upon Management to share information with their counterparts about their team activities. That way, the overall Quality effort can be monitored and managed in an unobtrusive way. Management can remove obstacles from the path of the teams before the teams even know that an obstacle would have existed.

Eventually, as the Quality process grows, the onus for cooperation and coordination begins to rest with everyone.

In many ways, cooperative and coordinated systems are analogous to choreography. As the Quality effort matures, teams and individuals can rest assured that, like a ballerina taking a leap, when they do step out with changes, there will be someone there to catch them.

Importance of People and Teamwork

One of the principal foundations on which Quality is built is that those people who actually perform the process are the ones who are most knowledgeable about it. Historically, we have made the mistake of thinking that managers were all-knowing and all-seeing—just because they had been promoted.

With the advent of team activities, we learned that, in fact, the Management level is usually the last to know. Team activities—both intact and cross-functional—are the basis on which improvement activities succeed.

Information flow changes radically in a Quality environment. As the implementation effort matures, it is soon apparent that information is much more available than before. Decisions are being made based on worthwhile data—not just an individual's previous experience or feelings. And those worthwhile data are shared with teams from other areas of the organization to ensure that no opportunities for suboptimization arise.

The more attention given to successfully working together by building cooperative and coordinated systems and relationships, the better the chance that the organization will ensure and improve its competitive position. Only by working together can we be assured that all aspects of the organization are working toward the same goals.

Pride and Dignity

Quality is the most humane thing to happen to organizations in at least a century. Over time, we have undervalued our employees at all levels to the extent that expressions such as "leave your brains at the door" have become commonplace. And this doesn't only apply to the lower levels of an organization. Management has been stifled and frustrated in many of the same ways.

In a Quality environment, we have the opportunity to regain our individual pride and dignity. By using our brains, we can give the organization what it needs, while at the same time, establishing a sense of personal satisfaction.

Each person in the organization must be valued for his contribution. By providing people with an environment in which they can contribute without fear, each individual is allowed to stretch and grow beyond any bounds they have previously known. And only by allowing people to strive and succeed can organizations continue to exist.

Regaining personal pride and dignity is not only a matter of humanity—it is a matter of survival.

CHAPTER 3

A History of Quality Implementation

Usually, when authors write of the history of Quality, they approach the subject chronologically. In those histories we get to read about Walter Shewhart and the folks at the Bell Laboratories; how World War II demonstrated to us that the West can successfully implement continuous improvement techniques; Deming's first and subsequent invitations to Japan; etc.

The purpose of this chapter is not to discuss Quality Management from the chronological perspective. Instead, this chapter presents an implementation history of Quality as it has been used—and abused—during the final quarter of the twentieth century.

The Five Waves

Historically, implementation seems to have come in five separate and distinguishable waves. The tack most organizations seem to have taken is that if one technique doesn't work, try the next one. What has been forgotten is that continuous improvement is a holistic approach to the organization. As a result, the organization should not move from technique to technique as if they are mutually exclusive, but treat each as a learning experience and determine the best strategy for combining aspects of all into a cohesive whole.

First, let's take a look at the Waves. Then, we'll talk about how to make the best of them.

Wave One: Quality Circles

First, there were Quality Circles. They began in the late 1970's—just after we began to realize that the Japanese had done something momentous—and we had missed it.

So, organizations began to establish Quality Circles throughout operations. The primary focus was on the manufacturing end. The structure called for "teams" or "circles" of employees to get together to discuss problems they had in their immediate operations.

Neither the teams nor the circles were well defined entities. They usually consisted of intact work groups of line employees who were given about an hour each week in which to discuss whatever problem they had chosen. Rarely was Supervision or Management included in the Circle process.

Also, "problem" was rarely defined—at least not by Management. The Circles were usually given free rein to identify and discuss any issue which they believed warranted time and attention.

This activity began the first wave of improvement-oriented training in the United States. Training organizations were mobilized to develop and deliver extensive training programs on group dynamics, leadership and facilitation, and problem identification and solving. Not a bad outgrowth of something which was ultimately mishandled by everyone.

So, here are the Circles. Employees spending time—sometimes a lot, sometimes a little—working towards the final goal: a presentation to Management.

Please note that the end goal was *not* the implementation of a corrective action recommended by the Circle. Therein lay the problem.

Management had unwittingly structured the Circle process to focus on a finish line which looked like a presentation to Senior Management. So with the end goal perceived to be a presentation, again the training organizations enthusiastically joined in, expanding their repertoire to provide presentation skills training to circle members.

Ultimately, we were left with a Management group which couldn't figure out why everything didn't change for the better. Hadn't they allocated the time for the Circles? Hadn't the training organizations provided an outlandish amount of time, training, and new skills? Hadn't they had to sit there and listen to those presentations—*ad infinitum?*

Worse yet, we were also left with an employee group which trusted Management even less than before. It didn't take long for the employees to decide that the presentation was being used as a sop by Middle Management to make Senior Management believe that there was support for the process.

Cynicism was given a new meaning.

So, we let the wave of Quality Circles come to a slow, quiet death. Some organizations allowed them to continue in one form or another. Most simply let them quietly go the way of any number of other "improvement programs."

Only, we didn't know quite where to look next. Clearly the

Japanese had Quality Circles. After all, we got the idea from them. Only they must have been doing something besides just allowing their employees to get together and sit around and talk.

But what did they do? They measured. Welcome to Wave Two: Statistical Process Control.

Wave Two: Statistical Process Control

The next belief we encountered was that if everyone learned everything about the basic tools of Statistical Process Control (SPC), then everyone would implement the tools and techniques in their work areas.

Quick — mobilize the training departments! Statistical Process Control was on its way! Only this time we would need some Subject Matter Experts (SMEs, by name) to give us the guidance to know what to teach.

Quality Assurance, Quality Control, Manufacturing Engineering, Industrial Engineering—finally, someone was going to listen. Finally, everyone would know how things should work.

And so, everybody learned how to do process flow diagrams, cause-effect diagrams, develop checksheets and—saving the best for last—CONTROL CHARTS.

Walls were papered by control charts which were generated by the Quality control areas with supposed assistance from the line workers. More often than not, if the line workers were asked just what those charts up on the walls in their work areas were supposed to show, they didn't have a clue. But, they did know that someone came around every week or so to change them.

Quality departments became responsible for "after-the-fact Quality," and, supposedly, real-time Quality as well. Data were collected religiously, reported up to Management and forgotten. No one's time was leveraged to focus on corrective actions. No systems for corrective action were instigated. Successful Quality began to be measured, not by the improvements which any department could report, but by the number of employees trained and the number of "Quality improvement projects" which were in progress.

Some organizations developed department and division rating systems to measure these so-called Quality activities. They usually consisted of a rating based on the ratio of employees or divisions or departments to the number of project activities. Often those project activities were defined as specifically as the number of process flow diagrams, etc. which had been generated; the number of control charts active in the area; the number of experiments (both classical and Taguchi) which were in process, and on and on.

What the rating systems didn't consider was whether or not these activities were needed, whether the data were of value, or whether anything was being done with the data. Yet, based on these data, careers were made and broken. Managers who could report large amounts of activity were highly regarded. Those who could not were often moved out of their Management positions.

Quality, manufacturing, industrial engineering, and training personnel were either feted for their successes in the training and implementation of measurement systems or blamed for the lack of dollar-reportable improvements in the organization. Unfortunately, it was usually the latter.

And, where were the employees through this wave? Most were sitting on the sidelines watching yet another one of those "programs" go the way of its predecessors. Some, who did become actively involved in the process, had the opportunity to develop an even stronger distrust of the organization. After all, this was the wave where real data were actually collected and reported. Finally, employees had the opportunity to see specific data supporting their long-held contentions about what the *real* operations problems were. They were vindicated.

Only they were also punished. One of the most compelling—and disturbing—outcomes of this wave, was that data were used as a means of justifying punitive measures between and against employees. Management quickly learned that they could use SPC data—real-time data—to build justifications for disciplining or laying off employees. Many managers used the data exclusively for that purpose.

Employees involved in the data collection process soon learned that they could sabotage the data collection system to show just about anything they wanted to show. There were instances of employees using SPC data to build cases against other employees who were not liked by their co-workers. It worked. And it was unrealistic to expect the Quality department personnel to be able to do anything about it.

These abuses of the system, unfortunately, occurred just about the same time that many organizations began laying off employees for reasons having nothing to do with Quality. To this day, many organizations are still suffering from the correlation which employees at all levels draw between anything to do with Quality and imminent lay-off.

A new obstacle was born. With all of the good intentions

in the world, the Statistical Process Control wave didn't work the way it was intended.

Just like Quality Circles, SPC resulted in some excellent findings about organizational processes and operations. It also resulted in corrective actions in many instances. But over the long term, it didn't result in the ongoing attention to improvement—which was the intent.

Why not? As with Quality Circles, it was because Management did not yet understand its responsibility in Quality implementation. To be fair, neither did the employees. And so, we moved on. This time we weren't going to make the same mistakes.

We did Quality Circles—and some of that was good.

We did Statistical Process Control—and when it worked it actually resulted in cost reductions.

What we didn't do was focus on how to get things done. Quality Circles worked, except Management wasn't involved. SPC worked, except we weren't adequately using employees. All we needed to do was combine the two missing links and what would we get? Culture Change!

Wave Three: Culture Change

This was a particularly interesting phase in the development of Quality implementation. In some respects it was a lot like going back to Quality Circles. In fact, many training organizations and consultants did just that. They went back to their materials from almost a decade before, slapped on the name Quality Cultures, and presented it to a somewhat new, but very jaded, market.

Now that we knew what went wrong with Quality Circles and SPC, we were sure not to go wrong with culture change. The reason? Because there was a mass consciousness which determined that in order to successfully bring change, it was necessary to alter the environment in which the employees worked.

This was done in a variety of ways. First we changed our language. Managers should no longer be "managers." They had to be *Leaders*. And eventually even that nomenclature changed. Eventually, they became *Coaches*. Some organizations even had contests allowing people to choose their own titles.

In order to view employees in the right light, they were no longer called "employees." They were now *Associates*. Some organizations which used the term *Coaches* even had employees referred to as *Players*.

Not a bad idea, overall. There is a long-standing and well founded theory which says that language determines culture. And so, following that logic, if we changed what we called our managers and employees, the culture change would begin to follow suit.

Right? Well, not quite. While we were more than willing to change our language, we did not make the corollary changes in the way we did business. So, what we were left with, in many cases, was a still-standing bureaucracy simply with different titles attached.

The second thing we did was to actively adopt the idea that bureaucracy was bad and flattened organizations were good. Suddenly the articles were filled with examples of improved efficiencies resulting from getting rid of the middle layers of the organization.

This, too, was a good idea. It also created one of the largest-looming and all-powerful obstacles Quality implementation efforts encounter. Why would anyone in Middle Management, and in their right mind, want to support an effort which is almost guaranteed to lose them their job? They didn't.

Thirdly, we began to look at the differing needs of employees. Cultural diversity in the workplace became a part of Quality consciousness. Differing styles of adult learning were discussed as a means of improving the effort. The psychology of change was introduced as a part of the need for understanding.

These were all excellent additions to the body of knowledge. They brought the humanistic aspect of Quality to the fore—something which had been missing in the previous waves.

So, it should have worked. Unfortunately, we were, again, unhappily surprised by the lack of overall success. What we had not considered was that by changing the words and pictures attached to the organization, we were not addressing the whole. Instead, we were only looking at those parts which seemed to be easiest to pick out.

This was the phase during which the expression "Walking the Talk" became most popular. The idea is good, but what happened to the phrase was indicative of this wave of implementation.

Managers on all levels talked about the need to "walk the talk"—with little to no understanding of what the talk was all about. Employees blamed managers for not "walking the talk" when, in fact, the employees understood little more than the managers about what was really entailed in this process.

"Walk the Talk" became the slogan of Wave Three—a frequently empty admonition and reminder that there was another one of those "Quality Improvement Programs" underway.

So, now where were we? We had tried working the cultural aspects of the organization (twice) and we tried measurement. We were still having a great deal of difficulty defining what our end-product expectations were. Where to focus next?

Wave Four: Customer Service and Satisfaction

Again, an excellent idea: to focus on our customers' needs in order to gain and maintain marketshare. Service is often a discriminating factor in our choice of which product or service to buy. So, service became the buzz word of the moment.

There were even measurement systems which could be attached to this area of focus. We could do surveys of our customers ("little buzz") and we could do benchmarking of organizations which we should consider emulating ("BIG BUZZ"). Both of these would provide important data from which we could make more knowledgeable decisions about the direction the organization should take.

On the customer service side, we focused on the front line. Service standards were established which were reported to customers to demonstrate the dedication of the organization to the customer needs. Customer service training returned. Employees who had contact with customers were trained to treat the customers right. The onus of success was put on the people who had the least amount of power to make it work.

What many organizations focusing on the customer were not taking into consideration was that in order to fully satisfy the customer needs, *it is first and foremost necessary to identify the customer's needs and then begin to address those needs through the internal processes of the organization.* Unless the processes and systems within the organization are set up to support the needs of the customers, those needs will be met, at best, for only a short time. When a new need is identified, and it will be, the organization will be unable to support a multiple focus unless actual improvements have been made to the internal workings of the operation.

In order to remain competitive, it is necessary to look both inside and out. The two needed to complement each other for this wave to succeed. In fact, the first and most important customer which must be satisfied is the *internal* customer. Only by doing so can the internal customer-supplier chain ensure that the external customers receive the products or services they expect, demand, and which are due them.

Wave Five: From Anything Goes to Integration

The fifth wave is the one in which organizations currently operate. It began with a preponderance of tools and techniques which were going to be the new answers to all questions. These ranged from the strategic (e.g., new visioning techniques) to the tactical (e.g., business process re-engineering). It has evolved into an understanding that Quality is necessary but that we still don't necessarily know how to define or achieve it.

In many ways, the fifth wave resembles its predecessors. As each new tool comes along, organizations hop on the bandwagon and begin implementing. Later they find out that the technique was not necessarily appropriate for or correctly applied to the organization. Unfortunately, in that way we have not necessarily learned from our past.

This wave has also been the wave of the apology. Theorists who were put in unfair positions as "Gurus" have had to come back and say that they were misunderstood or that they didn't realize the full impact of their theories on the organization. This has added to the level of distrust which already existed.

The most positive outcome of this wave is the understanding that Quality is a non-negotiable for the organization. Management and employees, alike, have come to realize that while they may not now be able to adequately define or implement Quality, they must somehow find a way to strategically define and consistently incorporate it into the operations.

It is hoped that this will be the last identifiable wave in the history of Quality implementation. It is one wave, even with the still existing confusion, which is marked by the understanding that Quality and continuity are linked.

Fast change and organizational flexibility are marks of Quality and can only be achieved through a rigorous commitment to continuous improvement. Continuity is defined through that rigorous commitment. As organizations improve in their levels of Quality strategy and process understanding, so, too, will their implementation activities improve and succeed.

Lessons Learned — and Recommendations for Action

It must be said that all five of the waves of Quality implementation contained a great deal of good. Organizations which worked these waves reaped rewards which remained long after the focus had shifted to another direction or improvement technique.

So, why didn't any one of them individually succeed? Because successful Quality is a compilation and combination of all five Waves—not just one or the other.

What we have done is to take each effort and superimpose its requirements onto the "real" work that people have to do. Again, we forget that Quality only succeeds when it is treated strategically.

Quality *is* the real work of the organization. Implementing Quality allows the organization to integrate the concepts of Quality and continuous improvement into the day-to-day operation.

Unless we treat Quality as the way we do business, we have upheld the cynicism and created "another one of those improvement programs."

It is the holistic approach to Quality which ensures success. So, what should we do? We should begin by analyzing and learning from our successes and mistakes in each wave.

Use the techniques and learning from Waves One and Three (Quality Circles and Culture Change, respectively) to address operational and cultural issues. Identify needs and opportunities among the employees.

Use the techniques and intent of Wave Two (Statistical Process Control) as a basis for measurement. Access the data which were and are being collected, determine what, in fact, the critical measurement points are, and move forward from there.

Focus on Wave Four (Customer Service) to get at how to identify and address customer needs. And use the learning resulting from Wave Five (From Anything Goes to Integration) as a means of making the combination of all the pieces make sense.

Use the applicable components of the waves concurrently. Don't delegate specific aspects of the process to different departments. Management is responsible, *in toto,* for the Quality effort. That means a combination of all that has gone before—and all that will occur in the future.

Quality, you will remember, is defined as *the unrelenting pursuit of continuous improvement throughout an organization which is realized by accessing and utilizing the concerted knowledge and experience of managers and employees at all levels in a data-driven, cooperative, coordinated, and systematic approach.*

If you review the waves, including assessing how you and your organization are coping with Wave Five, you will soon see that each is represented in the definition. It is the combination which creates a successful Quality effort.

In this case, the whole is much greater than the sum of its parts.

CHAPTER 4

Reducing Risk: Using the PDSA

The centerpiece of any continuous improvement implementation effort is the PDSA or Plan-Do-Study-Act cycle. In some circles it is known as the Deming Cycle for Continuous Improvement. Others refer to it as the Shewhart Cycle. Frankly, it doesn't matter what you call it—as long as it is the basis for all improvement efforts being implemented throughout the organization.

Plan

Whenever there is any idea proposed for an improvement of any kind the first activity that must occur is planning. The group of people who should be involved in the improvement effort must get together to discuss exactly what it is that they are looking at improving. Further, they must also discuss just what they want to do about it.

This is a definitional as well as a planning phase. Tools and techniques which are data-oriented must be employed at this point. Otherwise, how does anyone know what they are really looking at?

The importance of this phase cannot be understated. There is a tendency, once a problem or opportunity has been identified, to want to jump immediately to a solution. Full attention to the planning phase ensures that once a jump is made, it is made in the right direction.

In this phase, the team or teams meet, discuss the problem, identify various alternatives for corrective action and improvement, establish a plan of action, assign specific roles and responsibilities, develop or identify data collection systems, establish data collection duties, develop an action plan, and determine a representative time period. Only after all of that has been accomplished, do they then move to the next phase: Do.

Do

The next step of the cycle is to implement the plan of action which was established in the planning phase. The implementation activity is accomplished on a pilot basis *only*. The importance of this management limitation cannot be emphasized strongly enough.

The purpose of the PDSA cycle is both to identify improvement opportunities and methods *and* to avoid creating errors on a large scale basis. By implementing on a pilot basis, the organization is protected from potential large-scale errors.

If the team identifies methods of improvement, implements them on a large-scale basis, and then finds out that their action suboptimized or adversely affected the organization in some way, they have not implemented an extremely important aspect of the cycle—Damage Control.

The secret, if there is one, of the PDSA cycle, is that it takes those opportunities which have been identified for improvement and provides an implementation structure which encourages risk-taking while, at the same time, reducing the risk to the organization. As such, the team, in their planning process, must not only identify the actions to be taken, etc., but also how to implement them on a pilot basis to start.

This may cause some dissatisfaction among the team members. Often, those involved in the improvement process are so convinced of the infallibility of their ideas that they lose sight of the importance of the pilot. Management must convey their support for and belief in the team's activities at the same time impressing the importance of the initial limitation to the team members. Ultimately, this limitation supports the greater good of the team, the organization, and the Quality improvement process.

Study

This is the part of the cycle which was changed to address the penchant for "quick and dirty." The original name of the cycle — and one with which many are still familiar — was PDCA or Plan-Do-Check-Act. It was changed because we did just that. We checked. We did not analyze. We did not look below the surface. We took a quick and dirty look at what we quickly and dirtily implemented just to make sure it looked okay before reporting the results to Management.

It was quickly found that this, too, worked against the greater good. We must study the results of our efforts not only from the perspective of the immediate process implications, but also from the perspective of interactive effects.

Remember, the pilot is structured to minimize the risk to the organization. If the team members (and any outside resources they require) don't fully study the results of the implementation effort, an increased—and potentially destructive—risk is being created.

So, the team members must make time to review the results of their efforts, analyze the process effects, compare results against expectations, determine what, if any, unexpected occurrences or variables entered into the picture, and be prepared to make recommendations on next steps. Because the next step will be to Act.

Act

This is probably one of the least understood parts of the cycle. There are three alternatives from which to choose during the action phase. They are:

- Adopt the Change
- Alter the Change

or

- Abandon the Change.

We will examine them one at a time.

Adopting the Change

This action is taken if the team members are satisfied, after studying the results of their effort, that the corrective action or improvement recommendation worked. By their definition, the change was successful.

If this is the result, the team should then decide to adopt the change as is, maintain the improved process technique(s), and move directly into the planning phase to determine new improvement opportunities, or ways by which the newly implemented improvement can be expanded to other parts of the organization.

Thus, the improvement process cycle continues.

Altering the Change

This action is taken when the team is confronted in their study of results with variables or occurrences which had not been factored into the original plan. Maybe there were new employees hired. Possibly the time period for the pilot study was not representative. The team must identify what those variables or occurrences are and factor them into a redesigned plan. The greatest value of this Action is that the team has succeeded in collecting new and important information which allows them to redesign the pilot—still minimizing risk to the organization.

Thus, the team moves back into the planning cycle, re-designing the improvement effort taking the new data into account. Once new plans have been set, the improvement cycle continues.

Abandoning the Change

This is, undoubtedly, the least understood and potentially most impressive action in the overall cultural transformation of the organization.

Should a team decide, based on the data collected, that the improvement recommendation did not work, then it should be abandoned. This is a *learned* decision. It is based on rational analysis and study of the data while the pilot improvement was in process. It is one of the finest decisions a team can make to save their organization from disaster.

Too often, because of the way organizations operate, we tend to think only in terms of success or failure. When a team is faced with the "failure" of their recommended improvement actions, the team members react as we were taught to when we did not "win."

Unless Management takes strong, positive action to commend all improvement efforts—particularly those which lead to the decision to abandon—the teams will not continue the effort.

In fact, by determining on a pilot basis what the organization should *not* do, team members have saved vast amounts of money, time, morale and frustration. Let's face it. Usually when we have an idea which goes bust we are afraid to admit it, let alone broadcast it. In a true continuous improvement environment, team members must be applauded for recognizing a potential hazard to the organization before it was allowed to create havoc. They must know that in a PDSA-driven company, there is only positive recognition for those people who try.

Outcomes and Implications

When implemented consistently, the outcomes of applying the PDSA cycle are both problem-solving and problem avoidance. In either case, the organization is realizing cost savings through improved operations.

Teams are given the opportunity to actively participate in the improvement process. Middle Management is involved in, and understanding of, the improvement activities going on in their organizations. Senior Management is actually free to do the work they were hired to do—prepare the organization for the next stages of their strategic development and direction.

We talk about "flipping the pyramid" or pushing the decision-making to the lowest level. By structuring the improvement effort using the PDSA cycle, senior Management can realize the gains of ongoing continuous improvement at the lowest possible risk to the organization.

There is great strength and elegance in this tool which seems almost too simple. This is a structured methodology for continuous improvement which radically reduces the potential risk to the organization. Innovation and creativity can run rife through the organization with the assurance that whatever works—and whatever doesn't—will be tried, tested, studied, analyzed, and acted upon; all in a controlled environment.

For Middle Management, the watchword is control. By actively using the PDSA, and asking their teams to do so, Middle Management will know where the process lies, what the plan for improvement is, what the expected timelines are, how it's going...you name it. This measure of control will work to avoid the typical Middle Management concerns and obstacles. What have they to be afraid of if they are knowledgeable and in control of every aspect of the process as it occurs?

Finally, for the employees, the PDSA works to create a sense of accomplishment. These accomplishments are many and varied. They range from the exhilaration of being listened to—sometimes for the first time—to the enjoyment of involvement in a structured problem-solving opportunity.

Remember, most often the employees involved in the team efforts have wanted whatever is being corrected to have been taken care of long ago. As the owners of the process and the ones who work within that process each day, they have a vested interest in and positive outcome from making structured and accepted improvements.

Clearly it is in the best interests of all aspects of the organization to adopt and implement the PDSA as a way of doing business. It comfortably and easily translates continuous improvement into day-to-day operations as a way of doing business.

PART 2

Structuring Implementation

Introduction

There is a certain danger in including a section entitled "Structuring Implementation." Too often those who are implementing Quality are looking for someone to tell them exactly what to do at each step of the process.

Unfortunately, such knowledge doesn't exist—at least not unless someone has had the opportunity to analyze the organization and assist in developing an implementation structure.

The fact is, there is no such thing as a "cookbook" approach to Quality. Each organization must be responsible for analyzing its operation, determining the best strategy, designing and developing an implementation structure, and assessing whether what they have piloted is quite correct.

Sounds like the PDSA doesn't it? Funny thing about that. The best—and only—way to ensure success in Quality implementation is to use the PDSA as the model for implementation.

The next three chapters will provide you with a structure of outcomes and expectations for each step in the process. This is to be treated as a recommendation only.

As a result, while outcomes and expectations will be presented in each of the chapters, you will not be provided with the exact steps or techniques. There are a myriad of ways any one of these phases can be addressed and it would be both unfair and unethical to suggest the exact methods which would work in your organization. And so, you must begin as you mean to go on.

Study the organization. Assess its position in the market. Review the strategy in place. Identify a vision of where you want the Quality process to take you. And then begin applying the PDSA in each aspect of the implementation process throughout the organization.

Quality implementation is a phased and iterative process. As the organization learns more about itself, it knows better how to move forward. And, as it begins implementing its own phased approach, it may be determined that some of the activities suggested in these chapters belong in other spots along the way. Again, that's why—no cookbook.

If you are not in Management, but you are involved in the Quality process, discuss with your immediate and upper level Management the direction of the effort. Make sure that you and your colleagues understand what Management is looking for, what their strategy is, and how you fit into that strategy.

Remember, Quality is a cooperative and coordinated effort. Without reciprocity and free flow of information, you are likely to encounter a number of obstacles along the way which could have otherwise been avoided.

And if all of those pieces are not in place as you begin, maybe putting them in is where you should start.

CHAPTER 5

Assessment & Planning

The first phase of the Quality implementation process is an intense study and analysis of the organization's goals, direction, strategy and how the Quality process can be used to achieve the desired position in the marketplace. To that end, the objectives of the first phase include:

- Understanding the current culture, performance activities, and environment of the organization.

- Identifying areas of opportunity and a baseline of current performance.

- Establishing a Quality infrastructure at the Management level to develop and support the implementation effort.

- Beginning the process of gaining consensus and support within the organization.

This is a Management-driven phase. Other than support of the last outcome noted above, there is little involvement of anyone outside of Management. But all levels of Management must be involved during this phase.

By the end of this phase, the Management structure and direction will be in place. This does not mean that every manager will be in full knowledge or support of Quality theory or practice. Just like everything else in Quality, that is an iterative and dynamic process. Everyone—managers and employees, alike—must realize that Quality is just as much a learning process for Management as it is for the employees. In fact, much more so.

And so, by working the implementation process using a PDSA approach and controlling risk as much as possible, the organization moves forward on a basis somewhere between blind faith and absolute assurance. At the end of this phase, implementation will be the next logical step.

Some Caveats

A number of caveats must be addressed during this phase in order to ensure the highest possible value.

The first is an urge which must be suppressed: the tendency of Senior Management to want to make announcements—usually flashy ones—about the organization's intent to adopt and implement Quality.

This urge is manifest differently from organization to organization and from manager to manager, yet it shares the same outcome. When beginning Quality implementation, Management must realize that even though their intentions are good and they believe they have fully adopted the philosophy, they are presenting their "new idea" to a jaded audience.

Unfortunately, because of previous disappointments, employees are usually ready to condemn the process before they give it a chance. You really can't blame them. Remember, they've been exposed, in one way or another, to versions of

Quality for years. Why should they believe that this time will be any different from the last? Or the one before that? Or the one before that.

It works much to the benefit of Management, employees, and the Quality effort if managers first work through their part of the Phase One process and then present the new way of doing business to the employees. By strategizing the ways by which Quality will be included in day-to-day operations, employees can be presented with the initial steps of a *fait accompli.*

The second urge which must be suppressed is for Management to begin the implementation process before any assessment. Organizations are action-oriented. We look for the bottom line. We want to go, go, go.

Adequate time must be taken for the assessment and planning phase. Otherwise, all Management is doing is tampering. They are not fixing anything.

Do *not* begin the implementation process until there is a shared understanding of the purpose and method of the Quality implementation process. Remember, Quality is a business strategy. Use it as such.

Finally, don't limit the types of approaches used in acquiring the data necessary during the assessment process. Be open to everything from surveys to employee focus groups to review of existing data.

There are a variety of techniques designed to address everything from organizational generalities to employee specifics. Identify the needs for the assessment process and then begin identifying ways and means of developing the necessary data.

Understanding the current culture, performance, activities, and environment of the organization

The purpose of this objective is for Management to determine just how the organization currently operates. As always, there is a tendency to believe that these data are already known and accessible. Don't be misled. You'll be surprised at some of the answers you hear to what seem to be easy questions.

In assessing the current culture, start looking at the decision-making process. Examine the structure of the organization. How many levels are there? Are they formal? How many are informal? Who really makes decisions?

How are those decisions implemented? Or are they? Are there any trends in the implementation or lack thereof? Does the organization seem to adopt certain types of activities and not others?

How does information move in the organization? What are the formal information channels? What about the grapevine?

What is the real performance of the organization? Examine alternate performance-oriented data. What do the customers say? Are there any customer-service data available?

How are data reported? Who gets those reports? What is done with the reports? Are the data reasonable and logical? Do they provide value-added information? How are data systems developed? Who controls the data and data systems? Who collects data? How? What are the timeframes for the data collection and the data reporting?

As far as activities go, how are the systems and processes organized? Which departments are responsible for what? And within those departments, what is accomplished by the various processes?

How do the processes interact within departments? Across departments?

What is the internal customer-supplier system? Is there one? Do the people at each step know who receives their output and for what it is used?

Is there a trusting environment within the organization? What is the relationship between Management and employees? Between and within levels of Management?

Is there a tendency to assign blame? Are people—on any level—used as scapegoats? Is there a tendency to place a value on everything (i.e., good or bad, right or wrong, etc.)?

What are the values of the organization? What is valued? What is not? Does the Management group focus on ethics? Integrity? Honesty?

To what types of measurement indicators do employees work? Are they aware of those systems? Is there a performance appraisal and/or MBO system? How is it used? How is it managed? Is there a relationship between performance appraisal and salary increases? Is the relationship real?

This list of questions, comprehensive as it may seem, is only a beginning in developing an understanding of where the organization is now. These questions, and more, must be answered in order to provide a basis for accomplishing the next objective.

Identifying areas of opportunity and a baseline of current performance

By reviewing the collected data, Management has the opportunity to take a strategic look not only at the Quality process but also at the direction of the organization. This is the time for questions such as:

- What specific niche does the organization address?

- Does it excel in that market?

- What are the customers' perceptions of the products and services offered?

- How does the organization compare to its competitors?

  - Where do its products and services differ?

  - In what ways are they the same?

  - How do we learn from our competitors?

  - How have we implemented that learning?

- Is there a strategic plan in place for the organization?

  - How many years does it look into the future?

  - Are the plans realistic or arbitrary?

  - How was the plan formed? Who had input?

  - Who has access to the information included in the plan?

  - How, if at all, is the information included in the plan shared throughout the organization?

- Has the strategic plan been implemented?

- To what effect?

- How often and in what ways is the plan reviewed and revised?

This list is not comprehensive. However, by reviewing these questions, Management can then incorporate the results of the internal operations oriented data gathering to begin determination of the opportunities existing in the organization which Quality can and should address.

The improvement opportunities identified should be a combination of both long- and short-term goals. Those opportunities which relate to employee safety, or could lead to the early demise of the organization must be addressed first. Other improvement opportunities may be postponed for later action.

The results of the data gathering both for this objective and for its predecessor, also provide a baseline of current performance. Depending upon the rigor of the assessment, Management will know, more than ever before, where the organization stands.

By having those data, Management is then able to establish realistic rather than arbitrary goals about where the organization can and should be going.

Because Quality is a business strategy, the data collected in pursuit of this objective will have an impact on the Quality infrastructure and on the implementation effort. It is imperative that there be integrity during all phases of the data collection and reporting process. If there is not, the organization is again faced with tampering, not improvement.

Granted, holding up a mirror does not always present us with the picture we would like to see. But, unless we take a good look and really *see* ourselves and our organizations for what and where we are, there is no hope of achieving any of what we set out to do.

Establishing a Quality infrastructure at the Management level to develop and support the implementation effort

Unless Management establishes an infrastructure from which to manage the Quality process, anarchy is being built into the system. So is an immediate scapegoat.

Senior Management must review the information gathered in pursuit of the previous two objectives so that the infrastructure they design to support the Quality effort is based on data and not personal opinions with potential bias.

There are five primary aspects of the Quality infrastructure. They are:

- Understanding by Management of Quality theory as it applies to the organization.

- Development of a Quality Strategic Plan.

- Establishment of a Quality Implementation Structure which is in concert with the Strategy.

- Development and implementation of a Corrective Action Structure designed to respond efficiently and effectively to recommendations from the teams.

- Ongoing evaluation and improvement to suit the needs of the organization.

These five aspects create a structure from which Management can manage. They also form the basis of trust for the employees. As long as there is an infrastructure in place which is communicated to and understood by all managers and employees, everyone can work to the same expectations.

Understanding by Management of Quality theory as it applies to the organization

Please note. We're talking *applied theory* here. Not theory just for the sake of theory. You will recall that one of the basic principles of Quality is continuous learning. This is an example of learning which is gained, most frequently, outside the organization.

Senior Management, no matter how good their intentions, rarely have a complete understanding of what they've signed up for when they commit the organization to Quality. To be fair, they shouldn't be expected to know everything about it up front. But they must understand the basics of Quality theory in order to strategize and move the effort throughout the organization.

What can they do? Read books. Go to seminars. Listen to audiotapes. Watch video tapes. Find out about Deming, Juran, Peters, Senge, Hammer, Ohmae, and others. Determine the applicability of the information presented. Identify ways that the Management can adopt and manage to the structure of the theory.

Even if your intent is to implement one theoretical structure alone, you will learn more about what to do and not to do by finding out about the theories of others.

Remember that the purpose of this particular process is to understand the logical underpinnings which support the Quality effort. This information will assist managers in their ability to communicate and drive the Quality effort through the Middle Management ranks and into the employee organization. Unless you understand *why* you are doing what you are doing, you are tampering.

Development of a Quality Strategic Plan

Senior Management must coordinate the organization's overall strategic plan with that of the Quality effort. Keep in mind, the outcome of the Quality effort is to enable the organization to achieve the goals set in the strategy.

By reviewing the data obtained during pursuit of the first two objectives, Senior Management is usually presented with a very clear picture of the organizational priorities. They are also able to identify means by which the Quality effort can be structured to address those priorities.

The first priority is to look at the crisis points in the organization which must be addressed first. Identify those activities which must be pursued to ensure immediate safety and viability needs. Some of these will have existed for a long time. They are readily apparent and usually relatively easy to address.

The next priority is to look at the connection between customer requirements, perceptions, and the direction of the organization. This should include an assessment of competitive positioning and performance. This is also a logical point at which to begin active dialogue with the customer, if that is not already in place.

The Quality process will allow the organization to identify those points in the process which produce waste. In this case, waste may be defined as those activities which support products and services for which the customer has no interest and for which there is no new potential market niche.

The Quality Strategic Plan also provides the beginning of the shared understanding between levels of Management regarding the purpose and intent of the implementation effort.

One common obstacle is entitled the "Middle Management Balk." This obstacle can be reduced and possibly avoided if Senior Management includes Middle Management in the participation in and communication of the Strategic Plan.

The Strategic Plan should reflect the direction and needs of the organization. It should not be a long document, and it is not cast in concrete. Just like everything else, the plan is reviewed for possible improvement on an ongoing basis.

Unless an organization is flexible and can respond to the needs of the customers, it will not remain viable. Do not let the Quality strategy become another bureaucratic nightmare for the organization. Use the strategy as a guideline for understanding and a means of building towards and monitoring the implementation process.

Establishment of a Quality Implementation Structure which is in concert with the Strategy

The establishment of the Quality Implementation Structure is the point at which the Assessment aspects of this phase move into the Planning activities. Management must review the results of the assessment activities and design an implementation approach which addresses both the internal issues and the customers' needs.

One of the most common mistakes historically made by organizations when beginning Quality implementation was a shotgun approach with everybody involved from the very first. What those organizations learned was that this approach was expensive, had little return on investment, and was frustrating for everyone involved.

Instead, Management should look at a phased implementation approach. The phases should be based on the overall strategy. Determine what needs to be accomplished first. Second. Third.

To be realistic, Management should limit the areas of strategic focus to no more than five, but preferably three or four. Remember, the managers and employees involved in this effort will be new at it. If everyone is overloaded it will create anxiety which results in either paralysis or tampering rather than improvement.

In developing the implementation structure, training needs should be assessed. Given the area of strategic focus, what types of measurements might be used? Will there be a need for Management and/or team development training? What resources are available in the organization to provide that training? What needs to be accessed from outside?

This is the tactical portion of the strategy. Once you have a direction in place, you need something tangible and manageable in order to guide and monitor the effort.

Development and implementation of a Corrective Action Structure designed to respond efficiently and effectively to recommendations from the teams

It seems as if this objective is premature. In fact, it isn't. One of the most common reasons leading to the demise of Quality efforts was Management's inability—and sometimes lack of desire—to respond to recommendations.

Employees aren't stupid. If they see that, once again, there is no system in place, they aren't going to try very hard to implement Management's "new program."

By establishing a Corrective Action structure, Management is taking care of two issues at the same time. First, they are sending a clear message to the employees that they recognize their own responsibility to the process and have designed systems to monitor those responsibilities. Second, managers at every level will be able to monitor and respond to team activity throughout their organization in a timely manner.

A Corrective Action system doesn't have to be anything fancy. It can be a system of responses to teams. For example, some organizations adopt what is known as a 24/72 system. This means that teams are guaranteed that they will receive an acknowledgment from the immediate and also the affected manager (if they are different people) within 24 hours. Then, affected Management has an additional 48 hours to meet and develop an action plan for addressing the recommendation. That information is forwarded to the team by the end of the 72 hour period. Subsequent activities are also reported to the team, which has been provided a timeline for Management's activities and response.

A system such as this assures team members that their activities are being addressed and have not gone to waste. It also provides Management with a structure for managing their own activities in the Quality implementation effort.

There are many other means of addressing the Corrective Action system. It is up to the organization to determine the way which will fit Management's needs while assuring employees that their efforts will have top priority.

Ongoing evaluation and improvement to suit the needs of the organization

As with every other aspect of the organization, the implementation effort must be under constant scrutiny to determine ways in which it can be improved.

Observe the activities of the teams. Are they moving forward? What obstacles are they encountering? How are those obstacles being addressed? Or are they?

What about the strategic plan? Is it still in keeping with the needs of the customer? Has anything changed which should be addressed either in the strategy or in the implementation effort?

Is everyone receiving the training they need? How are the training resources being leveraged? Is there adequate coverage and development of measurement and individual/team skills?

Is the Corrective Action system working? Are recommendations being addressed in a timely manner? What are the results of those corrective actions?

As Management continues to learn about Quality theory and how it applies to the organization, how is that information being communicated?

Remember, it is not just pieces of the process which are identified for improvement. It is, for Management, the systems and processes within which the managers and employees work which must be relentlessly studied and analyzed for continuous improvement opportunities.

Beginning the Process of Gaining Consensus and Support Within the Organization

Okay, let's take a look at what we're up against here. We've got a group of middle and lower level managers who believe that if this thing works, they're out of a job. We've got a group of employees who have been this way before, didn't like it, and don't particularly want to go back. And we've got a group of senior managers who really believe that Quality is the way to go—or at least they say they do within the hearing of the most senior manager who really *does* believe it. And even the most senior manager might not be quite sure of exactly what he has just bought into.

A challenge? Yes. An insurmountable one? No.

During the Assessment and Planning phase, Senior Management is given the opportunity to learn both what Quality is from the perspective of the organization and to get a clearer understanding of just why the organization needs it. It is incumbent upon Senior Management to develop means of involving the next levels of Management in the process so that ownership is recognized and shared.

Senior Management will always own the bulk of the responsibility. But, without the support and involvement of the middle and lower levels of Management, Senior Management will never realize their vision for the organization. And that, really, is the purpose of vision and mission statements. It is a means by which Management can describe their intent for the organization in words which provide understanding, direction, and motivation for the organization.

Only, most organizations have vision and mission statements, and so what? They turn into little more than an advertising ploy trying to convince customers, suppliers, and employees that the organization is dedicated to the described ideals.

Vision and mission statements should not be beautifully framed and mounted on every wall—only to be forgotten. They should not be enclosed in each employee's paycheck for them to read if they get the chance.

Vision and mission statements must be living, breathing documents to which Management is held accountable. Teams at both the Management and employee levels should regularly review the vision and mission statements to determine whether the statements made are being upheld. If so, great. If not, these are opportunities for improvement.

Vision and mission statements are also excellent tools by which to determine if the team activities being proposed are in keeping with the overall direction of the organization. If it seems as if some of the team activities are going off on a tangent, that is the time for some additional analysis.

And vision and mission statements are not the only ways to establish consensus and buy-in. You should bring together different levels of Management to discuss strategy or implementation efforts at any opportunity. Senior Management must work with their direct reports to ensure that there is not only understanding, but a growing commitment to the Quality process. No one is exempt from Quality.

This is also a good point at which to review the results of the initial assessment information gleaned from focus groups. It may make sense to reconvene those groups and discuss ways by which buy-in can be improved. Some organizations establish cross-level teams specifically to analyze and monitor the consensus-building process.

Whatever it takes, it is not too soon to begin looking for both the obstacles and the supports for the Quality effort. That way, Management can begin to strategize how to work through the obstacles and capitalize on the support mechanisms.

If the Assessment and Planning Phase is taken seriously by the organization, Management and employees will both find that the logic and flow of the Quality effort makes sense and is workable. Ultimately, this phase represents putting in time up-front to avoid wasting time and effort in the midst of the effort.

CHAPTER 6

Implementation

This phase seems pretty self-evident. You've got a plan. You put together some teams. You have Quality. Were it only that simple.

The way to build success into the implementation phase is to come into it with the same eye towards strategy which took you through the Assessment and Planning phase. Only now the objectives are somewhat more tangible and the process is no longer just in the hands of Management. The objectives of the implementation phase are to:

- Improve profitability and customer relationships.

- Shift the organizational culture to Quality.

- Develop an organizational infrastructure to support and maintain ongoing success of the Quality effort.

- Train and educate personnel in the philosophy and techniques of Quality.

This phase is one of high emotion and drama for everyone involved. Barriers are being broken. Old models are being replaced with new, improved, workable solutions. Senior Management has the opportunity to see the realization of their overall strategic goals. Middle managers are allowed to utilize their expertise and not just push papers and people.

Employees are able to rid themselves of frustrations and impediments which have bothered them, sometimes, for years.

The drama is worth it because the results are magnificent.

Improve profitability and customer relationships

The funny thing about this objective is that it is the one which first drives most managers to enter into the realm of Quality. Yet it is, in many ways, the easiest to achieve. As soon as a team is let loose on an improvement opportunity, profitability will increase. It's almost unavoidable.

Think about it for a moment. Here is a group of people whose sole purpose is to analyze the work they do to determine ways of improving upon it while at the same time working to achieve the goals of the overall organization.

Not only will there be improvement of the immediate process, but there is usually a ripple effect. Functions which either affect or are affected by the process improvement area will have to be brought in to coordinate the support of the corrective action.

Internal suppliers must be brought in to discuss how they need to adjust their process to support the improved steps. Internal customers must have the opportunity to identify how the corrective action will affect their process area. As a result, both the internal customer and the supplier are intimately involved in the improvement process. They are, of necessity, improving their processes as a result of the initial improvement effort.

The issue of profitability opens up a number of questions which must be addressed during the implementation phase. It is both fair and necessary that employees become conversant with the financials attached to their process area.

Providing financial information serves two major purposes. First, one of the objectives of the Quality process is to turn each employee into a "businessman." That means that employees must have a knowledge of the profit and loss aspects of the process within which they work. By providing financial data to employees, they will be better able to strategize and make decisions about improvement recommendations and actions.

Some organizations have employees develop a forecast return on investment analysis for each improvement effort. As long as the employees are not held in any punitive way to the forecast, this information can be used as a guideline for both employees and managers about the potential financial outcome of the continuous improvement effort.

Second, by providing financial information to employees, Management is ensuring the sense of urgency necessary for a Quality effort to succeed. If the employees do not have other data, they will tend to believe that the Quality effort is being used as a cost-cutting mechanism which might result in layoffs and firings.

Remember, the employees work with a historical perspective about these things. The simple process of sharing information to inform employees about the status of the organization will establish a basis for trust and an urgency to do something to improve upon the current situation.

Third, given that Quality is not just a short-term fix and is, in fact, a business strategy, the focus shifts away from exclusively looking at short-term profits. Instead, knowledgeable managers begin looking at long-term potential based on the results of the Quality effort.

And who, besides the immediate organization, is benefitting from all this improvement activity? The customer.

There are a number of ways of addressing the customer relations aspect of the implementation process. Some customers want to be involved in the Quality process. They believe that by demonstrating their immediate support of the process they will have the opportunity to give input to the improvement effort. They also see this as an opportunity to learn more about the products they purchase so that they can better utilize those products now and in the future.

Some customers are not as interested in the day-to-day workings of the Quality process. For them, it is enough to know that the organization is pursuing a Quality effort. They believe, correctly, that they will benefit from those activities and are satisfied to sit back and simply enjoy.

Remember, organizations establish, in effect, partnerships with their customers. The relationship is one based on ongoing, mutual interest and benefit. As such, it is the responsibility of both the organization and its customer to discuss ways by which they can build cooperative and coordinated systems. An organization can only be assured of exceeding its customer's needs if Management knows what those needs are. It is the responsibility of both entities to make sure that that information is available and is being addressed.

Shift the organizational culture to Quality

Shifting the organizational culture, in any direction, is the responsibility and outgrowth of Management's actions. In a

Quality culture, as in any other, it is Management who sets the tone and must maintain constancy of purpose to ensure that it is not just a temporary adjustment, but a permanent shift.

The shift is towards cooperative and coordinated systems. Management must lead the organization in the direction set forth in the strategy. In order to do so, they must coordinate their efforts to ensure that they optimize the organization— and not go off on tangents.

Team efforts must be coordinated. Management direction must be consistent. Employees must know and understand that there is a direction in place and that everyone is working in that direction.

Some areas of the organization will shift more quickly than others. That isn't important. This isn't a race. As each manager and supervisor finds his feet in the Quality process, he will be better able to move his immediate organization in the necessary direction.

In some cases, the employees will take on the Quality culture faster than their Management. This can cause some dissent. Still, if the employees understand that there must be a cooperative system in place, they will also understand their role in assisting their immediate manager in moving in the Quality direction.

Systems to support the Quality effort must be developed. Some of these will be systems for continuous improvement which are implemented at all levels throughout the organization. Some systems will be exclusively at the Management level. All must be geared towards enabling the organization to move ahead efficiently and effectively.

The PDSA is, in fact, part of the culture shift. By managing and working the organization to the PDSA structure, the organization is adopting an alternate approach to its operations.

Culture shift is recognizable. As teams move through their development cycle, the shift in the culture towards cooperation and coordination will become apparent. Even the difficult phases the teams encounter along the way should be considered progress towards this objective being realized.

As Management begins the empowerment process, the cultural impact becomes apparent. Decision making is pushed to a lower level. Managers have more time to do the things they should do rather than those they have been forced to do.

The data collection and utilization process is also an indicator of culture shift. As the organization moves away from relying on opinions and moves toward utilizing data for decision-making, the culture becomes one which is data-driven and not oriented towards tampering.

There is an often heard lament during Quality implementation. That lament is, "How will we know when it's working? If it takes so many years to change the culture, then how will we know if there has been any movement at all?" By using the qualitative and quantitative data collected during the Assessment and Planning phase as a baseline, referring back to the strategic and implementation plans, and observing the behavior of the organization, Management will see the results of the Quality effort sooner than expected.

Just as with any developmental process, not all indicators will seem positive. However, if you take out the assessment of value and simply look at the movement of behavior, you will soon see that a great deal of change begins to occur in a very short period of time.

These are new data which must be tracked and analyzed in order to monitor and direct the future of the effort.

Develop an organizational infrastructure to support and maintain ongoing success of the Quality effort

This objective is the organizational equivalent of the Management infrastructure objective discussed in the first phase. In this case, it is the employees who are creating the infrastructure to implement the strategy as set forth by Management.

In establishing teams, the organization is, in effect, establishing the organizational infrastructure for Quality implementation. No matter what you call the teams, they are the mainstay of the ongoing success of the effort.

Establishing successful teams entails putting together groups of employees who understand the goals of the organization, the strategy set by Management to achieve those goals, the logic of Quality, and have the ability to utilize the tools and techniques necessary to accomplish those goals.

The teams must understand the goals of the organization in order to avoid tampering with the process, going off on tangents, or suboptimizing and potentially adversely affecting the efforts of other teams. They must feel themselves a part of the overall effort and have an understanding of what the ultimate goals are for the Quality effort.

In order to fully implement Management's vision, teams must understand the strategy set by the Management team.

This will give them their place within the context of the overall effort. It will also assist them in identifying other improvement opportunities which they or other teams might address.

The teams must understand the logic of Quality—that what they are doing is directly driven by a philosophy of which they must be a part. Management runs the risk of suboptimizing the Quality effort by focusing training exclusively on tools and techniques to be used by employees. Only if the team members understand, from a Quality perspective, the *what* and *why* of their activities, will they be able to work towards successful implementation of Management's goals.

Finally, the team members must have the ability to utilize the tools and techniques associated with Quality. There must be a focus on continuous learning so that the tools necessary are at hand whenever a team moves through a new or ongoing continuous improvement opportunity.

Train and educate personnel in the philosophy and techniques of Quality

This is where most organizations go wrong. There are far too many examples of organizations which decided to adopt Quality and instead implemented the most extensive—and expensive—training programs in the history of business.

Quality is not a training program. It is not Statistical Process Control, Conflict Resolution, Team Building, Leadership Skills, Problem Solving, Quality Function Deployment, Business Process Re-engineering, or any other single skill set. It is, in fact, all of them—and more.

With the appropriate skills and understanding in hand, employees will be able to work in teams and alone to improve their processes. They will work with their Management to identify new continuous improvement opportunities, culture shift opportunities, and opportunities to make recommendations about how the Quality process might manifest in the future.

Training must be strategic as well as tactical. It is incumbent upon Management to work with the training function to identify and implement only those classes which make sense. And, although it may be argued that the cost benefit of training cannot be measured, the positive financial outcomes of that training should be apparent through the implementation of the skills taught and learned.

Team members must be conversant with Quality theory as it applies to the organization and to their activities in particular. They must also have a working knowledge of the tools and techniques necessary to implement their particular process improvement activities.

Based on the strategy and implementation plans, the training department should be able to perform an adequate needs assessment to determine what skills will be required. That way, the organization can best leverage its resources to ensure smooth ongoing operations while at the same time realizing its goals for Quality, productivity, and profitability.

CHAPTER 7

Evaluation and Continuous Improvement

While this might seem as if it is the end of the process, it is, in fact, another beginning.

As stated from the first, the implementation process must be structured to follow the PDSA cycle to ensure success. That means that this phase really represents the Study and Act portions of the process. With an eye towards ongoing implementation, the objectives which an organization seeks to accomplish during this phase include:

- Analyze the Quality implementation effort for means of improvement.

- Identify additional Management indicators on Quality and productivity.

- Begin assessment of next phase requirements.

In achieving these objectives, the organization will benefit in a variety of ways. First, Management will have designed and managed a process based wholly on the PDSA structure. The process will have been used not only for the overall implementation but as a means for Management to practice using the continuous improvement structure as a management technique.

Second, all employees and managers will have had the opportunity to see Management demonstrate their commitment to the Quality process. They will realize the constancy of purpose manifest by completing a PDSA cycle. They will also trust more in Management's ability to understand their frustrations because Management will have experienced the same thing.

Third, the organization will benefit simply from the on-going analysis and assessment of the implementation process. This will be the time to take stock and determine how to go forward in an even more effective and efficient manner.

And fourth, because the teams will be more mature in their understanding of the Quality process, Management will have access to information and data previously unavailable to them.

Analyze the Quality implementation effort for means of improvement

This is the Study phase of the implementation cycle. It is at this point that Management must review all the data available which will act as indicators of the implementation process. For example, in which departments does the implementation effort seem to be stagnating? Flourishing? What is going on in those respective areas to create that result?

- What are the signs of culture change throughout the organization?
    - In what ways is the culture beginning to shift?
    - In which direction?

- How are the measurement systems working?
    - What new data are being reported?
    - How are those data being used?

- What is the status of the corrective action response system?
    - What is the level of satisfaction among both employees and managers regarding the system's structure?

- What shift, if any, has occurred in the structure of the organization?
    - How has that affected the organization overall and the implementation efforts in particular?

- How are teams being formed?
    - What are the criteria for team membership?
    - How were those criteria developed?

- How are decisions being made?
    - How is the empowerment process manifesting itself?
    - What can be done to improve upon that process?

- Which individuals seem to be having difficulty with the Quality concepts?
    - What training have they attended?
    - What can be done to assist them in their understanding?

- How has the training been structured?
    - On what basis is skills training offered?
    - How have managers leveraged the time of their people to maintain daily operations requirements?

- What is the current status of the organization's strategic plan?
  - How has the Quality effort supported Management's direction?
  - How can it be improved?

Unfortunately, there is also a need to ask questions about potential sabotage of the effort. Realistically, the people actively working the processes know better how to end-run the system than anyone in Management. As a result, quiet sabotage of the Quality effort is not an unknown occurrence.

If there is any thought that that is the case, the following questions might apply. Are there any indicators of sabotage of the effort from within the organization? How is that being done? Have those attempts been successful? What can be done to stop it?

This phase is reminiscent of the initial queries about the state of the organization. The data acquired during that phase are now the basis of comparative analysis.

This process, in some form, should actually be ongoing throughout the implementation effort. Don't wait for some arbitrary time period to first sit back and discuss how the implementation effort is working. Instead, early in the assessment phase, identify criteria which will be used as indicators throughout the Quality implementation process. Management should regularly review the status of the effort—separately and together—to identify opportunities for improvement.

It may also make sense to establish a team of workers to look at the effort from their perspective using the same and different indicators. Some organizations establish cross-level teams specifically for that purpose.

Depending on the trust in the organization, this may work. If, though, the trust level between Management and employees is such that free flow of communication would be hindered, access the data from each level separately and compare the results. Ultimately, using those results as a basis for discussion, a cross-level team might be established.

Identify additional Management indicators on Quality and productivity

Face up to it. Most organizations use indicators which give little to no real information on the status of the operation. Management spends more time in the dark as a result of the information they receive than they would if they were left to their instincts and observations.

Some of that continues in the early stages of the Quality effort. There is a tendency to establish new measurement systems, indicators, and criteria without determining whether the existing data provide any value.

At this phase in the implementation process, Management must review the data they receive and determine whether those data provide them with the information they need to make well-founded decisions.

You will recall that one of the principles of Quality is to build on the best. In this case, make sure that no existing data systems are thrown out simply because they were in place before the Quality effort began. It makes no sense to develop a new data collection and reporting system where a viable one already exists.

If, however, it is determined that an existing data system does not provide value-added information, do not speak negatively of that system simply because it is no longer viable. Remember that any system which is in place was put there in response to a need at the time it was developed. That need may no longer exist. That doesn't make the value of the system suspect. It simply makes the ongoing support of that system a potential point of waste in the organization.

It is also at this stage that Management should take the opportunity to find out what data are being collected throughout the organization and which they do not receive.

What data do the teams collect? What are the critical measuring points which have been established in the various processes? Will those data be useful to the Management team? How can those data be accessed?

How are the teams using the data to make decisions? What are the opportunities, based on the available data, its integrity, and the success of the team using those data, to expand the empowerment of the team members? What are the opportunities to share the data with other areas which might benefit?

The purpose of this review process is to determine ways of improving the team and Management decision-making process at each step along the way. Now that it is no longer necessary for decision-making to be based on opinions, at the very least the data should have integrity and be available where those data will do the most good.

Begin assessment of next phase requirements

Quality is a phased and iterative process. As such, it is the responsibility of the organization—Management in particular

—to determine the steps by which the implementation effort will flow most logically and smoothly.

As a result, there must be a review of current and historical data to begin determination of next steps. The strategic plan must be reviewed to ensure that the direction of the organization remains consistent—if, in fact, it should remain so. Once that determination has been made, the process to develop an implementation plan for the next phase begins.

Customers and suppliers should be contacted. Data from their perspectives should be included in this assessment. Competitive analysis and positioning should be reviewed and assessed. New markets should be considered.

It may go even further than that. This might be the right time to begin strategizing how to get customers and suppliers actively involved in the Quality process.

At some point there will be a need to bring the suppliers into the process. This has to be carefully strategized to ensure that the data provided to suppliers will have value and integrity. As well, it is important to remember that your suppliers are very likely supplying to your competitors. Without asking them to violate any confidentiality, a great deal can be learned simply by listening to their industry knowledge and perspective.

Dumping problems into the suppliers' laps must be avoided at all costs. Rather than blaming the suppliers, the organization must work with them to build a mutual understanding of processes and needs.

The goal of that collaboration is to build cooperative and coordinated systems between the organization and the suppliers. This will reduce costs, waste, and frustration for everyone.

On the customer side, a review of the marketplace should be pursued. Customers, both immediate and ultimate, should be polled to determine what additional products and services would improve their perception of the organization.

For the internal organization, the phased implementation approach means that decisions must be made regarding where new teams should be developed.

Depending upon the results of the first teams' efforts, you may be able to be assign new activities to existing teams. In other cases, altogether new teams must formed. In either case, the training department must be ready to go.

This is also a point at which decisions about life-cycles of teams are made. Some organizations choose to break teams into life-cycle oriented groupings. For example, a team which is ongoing is referred to as a "continuous improvement team." One which is issue-specific and will be disbanded at the conclusion of its efforts is referred to as a "process improvement team." And one which is to form and disband within an extremely short time period to address a crisis is referred to as a "tiger team."

Other organizations establish what are known as "self-directed work teams" among the intact work groups. Efforts which are cross-functional or in any way separated from the intact work group are named for the process or improvement project on which they are working.

If there are concerns about team life-cycles, be prepared to analyze the organization's needs and make recommendations based on available data. If the life cycle of teams is not an organizational issue, don't make it one.

The point is, Management at all levels has to be able to guide the team process whether it is for a long- or short-term effort. As such, they need to have the same understanding of the team requirements across all departments and levels of the organization.

Sometimes Management makes announcements to the effect that every employee must be involved in a team. This leads to questions among managers and employees regarding whether every person has to be actively participating in a problem-solving or process improvement effort all the time.

It's a touchy subject. On the one hand, the continuous improvement process is everyone's responsibility. On the other, if a particular process is not a strategic focus area, it may be premature and potentially dangerous for that area to begin implementation.

Management must be clear about the strategy and implementation steps which are taken. As the implementation process progresses, these types of issues tend to take on a life of their own.

It is at this point in the Quality process at which the Human Resources function becomes a key player in the ongoing success of the effort.

As the Quality effort matures, questions about performance appraisal, compensation, bonus, pay-for-education, and promotion systems arise. This even extends to questions regarding commissions for sales personnel. As the employees become more educated about the Quality philosophy, they will be looking for equity in the compensation and other systems.

Human Resources must be ready to address these issues in a timely manner and in keeping with the Quality philosophy.

Management will be looking at the Management by Objective (MBO) system to determine whether the goals are arbitrary. If so, they are in violation of the Quality philosophy.

Again, Human Resources must be ready to address those issues and many others. If they do not, the effect will be quick and deadly. Trust will once again be destroyed. Any steps which have been made in breaking down barriers between and within organizations will reverse. And the organization will ricochet backwards much further and stronger than before.

This is to be avoided at all costs. Once people are exposed to the joys of working in a Quality environment, they are unwilling to accept less.

In assessing next steps for each aspect of the implementation and improvement process, Management and employees should step back and analyze progress and obstacles. At that point the classic "Act" phase decisions should be made. Specifically:

- Which aspects of the process should be adopted as they are currently being implemented?
  - How can that corrective action be expanded to benefit other parts of the organizations?

- Which implementation activities should be altered as a result of new data?
  - How should a new corrective action recommendation system be structured for pilot?

- ■ Which aspects of the process should be abandoned and considered a successful lesson learned?
  - How can the data obtained from these efforts be used to begin the Planning phase once again?

As you can see, after reviewing the complete process, there can be no finish line in the Quality process. No sooner are improvements made to the system than there must be a concerted effort to determine how to build on those improvements and move even further.

There's a kind of comfort in knowing that no matter what you do, as long as you maintain the integrity of the effort, you can do no wrong. There is no blame placed because there is no need for blame.

We talk about a Quality culture and creating the right environment as if they are some amorphous "I'll know it when I see it" entities.

Not so. The three phase implementation process, supported by appropriate individual and team development, and managed closely by those in charge is exactly what you are trying to create.

No secrets, but no miracles either. Just an organization that operates exactly as you, your employees, and your customers and suppliers would wish.

PART 3

When Things
Go Wrong

CHAPTER 8

What to Look For

Something is wrong.

You have teams. You have measures. You even followed the PDSA process in establishing the improvement process. Still, something is wrong. You're not seeing the results you expected by this time—no matter what time it is.

The teams all meet but the recommendations they make—when they make them—don't seem to be addressing the real issues inside the organization. Things are moving—you're just not sure where.

You're right. Something is wrong.

The improvement process is one which, because of the complexity of the organization, can easily get misled, even with the best intentions of all involved. Sometimes, Management is able to clearly predict or at least identify when something is going wrong. Other times, there is that visceral feeling—almost intuition—that things are not working out as planned.

Either way it goes—by data or by gut—don't ignore the situation. In most cases, the problem will not take care of itself. And, in some cases, you might be surprised by the amount of progress made—sometimes in areas where you least expect to find it.

Indicators of a Process Gone Astray?

In most organizations, Management has some expectations regarding return on investment for the improvement initiative. In some theoretical camps, this is heresy. In an organizational culture, it is a Management safety net.

One of the ways to identify whether the improvement effort is netting any gains is to review those indicators from a number of perspectives.

Managing by Results

The majority of Management indicators are results oriented. They report what happened after the fact. For example, quarterly sales results report what happened in the preceding quarter. Based on those numbers, decisions are made regarding everything from staffing to inventory.

Yet, does anyone know—*really* know—how or why those numbers were achieved? It's doubtful. Yet, based on those numbers, careers can be made or broken.

If it was a good quarter, increased orders will be made for the items sold. Sales staff will be highly compensated for their performance. Everyone will be congratulated and very little may be done to analyze and assess how it became a "good" quarter.

If the quarter wasn't as good as expected, staff may be reduced. Commission structures may be recalculated to provide higher profits to the organization with less pay for the staff. Inventory levels may be adjusted.

And, throughout, someone in Management will be asking

"Why?" What happened to make it a "bad" quarter? What could the sales staff have done which would to ensure higher sales? Why do sales and other organizational performance forecasts seem to be just so much fantasy?

This scenario is no different from Management's expectations of teams. A team is set up and deployed. Expectations are created. The team will be the answer to all questions—or, at least they'd better be. Managers forecast that their teams will reduce inventory, increase productivity, decrease operating costs, *ad infinitum.*

Yet when the teams are deployed, little information is given to them about the costs of their operation, the strategic and tactical needs of the organization and their particular function —sometimes, even why the team was chartered altogether.

Still, the team continues to meet. They actively work on process improvements—some of which they can affect, most of which they cannot. Soft and best guess indicators are reported back to Management. Management becomes disheartened. Somehow, with the best intentions, the Quality process just did not work. And, what's worse, promises were made about team outcomes which didn't come true.

Now managers are put into a position of feeling that they must once again prove their worth to the organization.

"—No more teams.

—No more soft stuff.

— Let's get back to the real work of the organization and forget this Quality buzz!"

Management by Activity

Conversely, some organizations don't look to the bottom line for results. Instead, the amount of activity pursued is used as the ultimate indicator of the initiative's success.

Many organizations establish arbitrary indicators of success based on the number of teams, personnel involved in the initiative, number and types of measures, etc. If anything, these activity-oriented measures create more misunderstanding and havoc than those previously mentioned.

Senior Management must work with the truism that among their direct reports, "whatever is of interest to my Management is fascinating to me."

Now look where that gets you. If the Senior Management measure of Quality success is based on the number of teams established and the number of personnel involved in those teams then they will get exactly what they asked for—lots of teams with lots of people involved.

If Senior Management measures Quality success by the number of control charts, Pareto analyses, and designed experiments, then they will also get exactly what they asked for—control charts, Pareto analyses, and designed experiments.

The fact that none of these teams, people, or analyses is tied to any of the organization's strategic or tactical goals is immaterial. Well trained managers know that their success is based on the perception that they support their Management's initiatives and beliefs.

So, Management gets what they asked for. And, for many organizations, this turns into a case of "be careful what you ask for because you might get it."

Realistically, there will come a time when Senior Management will need to assess the investment made in this activity-based Quality effort. Did the teams work? Has there been a return on the investment made in the improvement initiative?

Chances are, the answer to these questions is "no." And what's worse, Management has just jumped the line from setting up criteria based on measuring by activity to assessment by the classic results indicators. And so, the disbanding process begins again. The Quality effort was a failure.

"—No more teams.

—No more soft stuff.

— Let's get back to the real work of the
organization and forget this Quality buzz!"

Sound familiar?

Managing by Corporate Edict

In many cases, managers find themselves responding to a little understood—and often not well defined—corporate edict:

"Thou shalt implement Quality."

That's fine as far as it goes. The problem is that quite often managers don't believe that they are responsible for, or are not given the opportunity to understand, what that edict actually means to them. In most cases, there is no definition of what is to be implemented anyway.

We're not talking only corporate giants here. Sometimes those corporate edicts come from the main office—which might be one building away from the location where the implementation is expected to actually take place. Sometimes it's the office next door.

This scenario creates a great deal of difficulty from the first. An immediate series of questions which arises usually includes:

- What is the home/corporate/parent organization, itself, doing to implement Quality?

- Why is it that *we* are asked to change how we do business but it seems as if *they* don't have to do anything differently at all?

- How are we supposed to provide all the off-line time for training and team activities when we are still being held to the same levels of productivity and, in fact, the same indicators?

These are fair questions, ones usually not taken into consideration when the Quality process is managed by edict.

Even with the assistance provided by the parent organization, whether it be training, consulting, education, or anything else needed, the corporate entity must first look to itself and to its intent before issuing the edict.

Understand that there is nothing wrong with the edict in and of itself. The difficulties arise if inadequate planning and analysis is performed prior to issuing the edict.

Remember, once the implementation process is in place, it should look seamless to those involved in its day-to-day activities. And the only way anything looks easy is for it to be preceded by a lot of hard thinking and hard work.

Balancing Activities, Results, and Edicts

In order for the organization to increase and improve its progress in the Quality initiative, it is necessary to create a balance between activities, results, and edicts.

The most Senior Management—on-site or distant—must commit themselves and the organization to an improvement initiative. Teams need to be established. Measures must be applied. The bottom line must be affected.

Yet, it must be understood that by implementing Quality, the organization is committing to doing business differently than it did before. This means that the rules have changed. Some initial understanding must include that:

- The vision and mission—as a reflection of the strategy and goals of the organization—must act as a homing beam, providing all managers and employees with a clear set direction.

- Managers at all levels must expand their repertoire to include managing to the vision and mission— and therefore to the organization's strategic intent— not just to their department's immediate goals.

- Classic results indicators can tell only part of the story.

- There are alternative ways to view the organization's operations which focus on process rather than exclusively on results.

- No matter how well targeted the team's activities, it takes time to understand, let alone change, how a process works.

- Management must become generous with information—whether strategic or financial—so that the teams can create the success the organization needs.

- It took a long time to create the current situation. It will not be an overnight trip to a well-operating organization.

This is not to say that organizations should sit back and simply wait for something to happen. On the contrary, a well-targeted, well-supported improvement initiative will net the organization gains in a short time period. And that's exactly where Management should start.

Reassessing the Effort

Let's return to our data-based or visceral belief that something has gone wrong. Where to go next? Managers can reassess the direction of the effort by asking the following questions:

- Are the teams' activities tied to our strategic goals?

- Have we done an adequate job of communicating the organization's needs?

- Have we communicated how each particular team fits in to address those organizational needs?

- What information have we, or have we not, provided them to assist in their efforts?

- Do measures exist which can adequately track the team's progress or do alternative Management indicators need to be developed and used?

- Does an adequate support structure exist to assist the teams in achieving its goals?

- How have we defined success among our managers?
  - Are we asking for, or receiving, unrealistic forecasts of the teams' outcomes?
  - Do we focus only on the surface measures (e.g., numbers of teams, analysis techniques being used, etc.)?

- What was our original intent in establishing the Total Quality initiative?
  - Have we maintained that intent?
  - Has that intent changed?
  - How can we improve the organization's understanding of the need as well as the intent?

- Are the vision and mission being used and discussed by Management and staff—or have they turned into attractive wall decorations?

Management may be surprised by some of the answers to these questions. Often, teams are working very well and, in fact, achieving the organization's goals. The problem is that Management isn't reviewing the process indicators which would give them that information. Sometimes the teams need just a slight adjustment in their direction to put them directly on track.

However, if it is found that the teams are far off base, then there has been a breakdown in the Management process. Somehow, the managers who oversee those teams' activities either lost sight of—or never had an understanding of—the purpose and needs of the improvement initiative.

Either way, the organization will simply need a dual effort approach—one to redirect the teams and one to better support the developmental needs and understanding of the managers.

The main thing is—don't give up on the Quality initiative. Remember that it, too, is included in the organization's *unrelenting pursuit of continuous improvement.*

The payback on improving the improvement effort will be substantial. Employees will see that Management is willing to admit to mistakes and correct them in a positive and supportive manner. The organization will understand that nothing is exempt from improvement. Further, a precedent will be set that as the organization grows and changes, so will the improvement initiative grow and change.

Managers will better understand their role in the new way of doing business and will work toward the long-term needs of the organization. And Senior Management will net more than they expected from the improvement effort—no matter what measure they use.

CHAPTER 9

Making Prior Efforts Make Sense

When organizations enter into the Quality effort, they rarely make use of some of their greatest information sources as a means to create success: prior efforts. Organizations have been involved in improvement initiatives for so long that many organizations have funds of directly applicable information available. For those industries who are just entering into the fray, they have the experience of those who came before as well as their own alternative resources to review. No matter at what point the organization's improvement initiative lies, it is important to review what has gone before to better understand how to predict the twists and turns of this newest effort.

Assessing Past Attempts

For those organizations which have what they consider to be "failed" efforts in their pasts, the assessment and review process is crucial. So-called "failed" efforts create a number of known and hidden results. Many of those results provide important insight into the way the organization responds to proposed change.

Placing Blame

No one likes to be a failure. No one likes to admit to being less than successful in anything they attempt. Put that scenario into an organizational setting with careers resting on the outcomes, and the results can be frightening.

Quality, no matter which wave has been implemented, has provided many opportunities to shift blame while running for cover.

"It was the Human Resources Department's fault. They didn't understand our people's needs and abilities."

"It was the Industrial Engineering Department's fault. They used measures which didn't make sense for what we were trying to do. Even worse, they wanted our people with their limited capabilities—to do an Industrial Engineer's work."

"It was the Quality Department's fault. We wanted to make improvements but instead of helping us, they kept acting as policemen."

"It was the Corporation's/Home Office's fault. They just dumped this thing in our laps without any why or wherefore —or without doing any of this themselves."

And, finally, "It was Management's fault."

- "They didn't give us adequate support."

- "They never made it clear what we were supposed to be doing or why."

- "When we did come up with answers they never listened to us anyway."

- "They run the organization—why don't they do something about it instead of dumping it on us!"

In each case, there is some truth to the matter. Historically, Management found that when the effort was delegated to any single department as their responsibility, the initiative didn't work.

As previously noted, the implementation waves which we have experienced weren't wrong. The mistake was that a mutually exclusive approach was being taken to address a multi-dimensional need. So, neither human resources, nor engineering, nor Quality, nor any other specific department got it right. There was no way that they could.

Of necessity, they looked at their newfound responsibilities from the perspective particular to their organization. Each had its own frame of reference which included its own definition of what constitutes "success."

And, as for Management, with the best intentions in the world, some of their mistakes have become the stuff of which legends are made. So have many of their successes. In both cases, deservedly so.

Yet, if you look at all of those blaming behaviors, you will note that they apply not only to the Quality process, but to most any other change for which implementation in the organization has been attempted.

Alternative Views

Think about the last time you implemented a new benefits program.

Management actively seeks best values for the organization as well for as the employees. Some of these might include co-payments, some might not. Health benefits for employees, their spouses and families, savings and retirement plans, possibly even a profit-sharing plan—they're all included.

The announcement is made. A new benefits package—better for the employees and the organization—is being implemented. Then—Take Cover!

No matter how well planned, researched, and executed, managers and employees at all levels will be actively taking up verbal arms against the plan.

- "How could they do this to us?"

- "It was so much easier the old way!"

- "They say that our benefits are being improved, but they're really not. It's just a way for Management to cut costs."

- "Some savings plan. Remember when there were matching funds—and no requirement to buy company stock?"

- "How about that profit sharing plan? Right. Now my bonus is dependent upon a bunch of people I don't even work with!"

And so it goes. The complaints. The reluctance—and sometimes refusal—to return necessary forms by the due date. The havoc created with only one intention in mind—to improve the working conditions for the organization and for its employees.

Whether you're implementing a new benefits package, updating computers, machinery or equipment, establishing new ways of tracking performance, or even holding meetings for all employees to provide them with up-to-date organizational information, it doesn't matter. Organizations have developed a low level of trust regarding mandatory change.

Does that mean that the organization should put itself into a permanent state of stasis? Not unless it intends to permanently close its doors—and soon. Instead, Management must look at what has gone before as a means of improving what will come in the future.

Using Past Experience as a Guide

The patterns demonstrated in the response to a new initiative can often be predicted based on the way the initiative is planned and executed. By reviewing how other new ideas were incorporated into the organization—as well as the pattern of response—Management will be giving itself a head start in either beginning or improving upon the Quality initiative. And if this sounds like the PDSA, it is.

Introducing a New Idea

Management must begin by asking questions specific to the planning and introduction of the initiative or change to be implemented.

- When the new initiative was being introduced, how was it done?
    - Was it in print or in person?
    - Who made the announcement?

- What preceded the announcement?
    - How, if at all, were employees involved in the decision-making process leading to the new initiative?

- What education was given to managers and supervisors prior to implementation?

– What training was provided to ensure that they would be able to easily answer employee questions?

The needs of the managers and employees in the area targeted for Quality implementation must be considered when planning the concept's introduction.

Should Senior Management meet with the department to discuss what is scheduled to occur? Should the message come from a more immediate manager who is known and held in high esteem by the employees in the area? What kind of support or corollary print materials should accompany the announcement?

Who should be involved, even before the announcement is made, in assessing the area's introduction and implementation needs? Who will be seen as having the best interests of the area—and not just themselves—at heart?

What can be done to prepare the managers and supervisors for the meeting? What are the most likely questions they will be asked after the meeting for which they must be prepared?

Overall, how can we create a smooth, balanced approach to the introduction and implementation which will reduce fears across departments and organizational levels?

Reviewing the Attack

Remember those verbal calls to arms? Even they have a great benefit for better understanding the needs of the Management and staff. Rather than simply hoping that the same thing will not happen again—after all this is a different initiative than the one before—the organization must take a close look at the substance of the attacks.

- Are there any common themes in the responses to new ideas?

- What seems to be of greatest concern to the managers and employees in beginning a new initiative?

- What differences exist on a department-by-department or area-by-area basis?

- Do we need to be prepared to explain the idea and implement the initiative in multiple languages?

- Have we tied the initiative to a clear understanding of the organization's needs and goals?

- Have we structured the initiative so that it is a win-win for all concerned—and that everyone can see it as such?

Remember, the Quality process is one built upon the premise that each employee at every level is working for the good of the organization. It is no one's intent to close the operation down—that would be working against their own best interests. Therefore, it is the responsibility of Management to invest in an initial and ongoing understanding of how the organization works and how to make it work better, attacks or no attacks.

Quality is not about right or wrong. It is simply and always about better.

Gaining and Keeping Control

Okay, the process is in place. Teams have been deployed and good things loom on the horizon. But how does Management balance the need to know how the teams are doing with the equally important need to monitor them—and not violate their trust in the process?

You will recall that an infrastructure must be established. The infrastructure is designed to address both Management and employee needs. No matter where you are in the process, this would be a good time to review that infrastructure to identify areas of improvement.

Understanding the Infrastructure

The Quality infrastructure is a Management owned and controlled device designed to monitor and support the improvement initiative. In its simplest terms, the infrastructure includes the management systems needed to oversee the Quality effort.

These management systems range from the ways that teams are decided upon and deployed to the ways by and the extent to which teams make decisions. Corrective Action systems are included in the infrastructure.

The infrastructure contains the management owned and guided systems which oversee the direction, intent, activities, and results of the Quality initiative.

Communication Systems

Management owns the organization's formal communication systems. All the documented traces of the organization—everything from policies and procedures to organization charts and lunch schedules—come from the Management structure. Technically, employees know what they know about the operation of the organization from the information provided them by Management.

In fact, the informal network (i.e., the grapevine) is far more knowledgeable and efficient than any formally run communication system encountered. There are a number of reasons for this. One is that the information moved along the grapevine is of far more interest and perceived impact to the employees. Another reason is that the information network consists of liaisons throughout the organization who, both in and out of their formal jobs, act as information conduits across departments.

There is no reason why Management cannot learn from the informal communication system and use it as a means of improving the formal communication network. For example, by identifying the people who act as liaisons in the organization, and building them into the improvement initiative, Management is assured that information about the Quality process—or anything else—will move forward. Or, by polling the liaisons to determine what is of real interest to employees, Management will be better able to target that audience and create interest in the initiative.

One of the other benefits of the informal network is its responsiveness. Employees who get their information from the grapevine can always get answers to their questions and they know that more information is on the way.

The conventional wisdom is that Management has no access to the grapevine. It is believed by managers that no information would be moved to them simply because of their position. In fact, employees are more than pleased when their management wants into the grapevine. It demonstrates that the managers are interested not only in the party-line, but also in the real feelings and activities in the organization.

There is a caveat, however. When Management accesses the grapevine, it must be done in a way that is information-seeking only. Employees will be wary of and on the lookout for the possibility that Management is attempting to spy on or present misinformation to the employee population. Managers must access in but not place judgement on the information gleaned.

The formal communication network, in contrast to the grapevine, has an information flow which is unidirectional—downward. Even if there are questions about the information provided, there is little belief that an answer will be given. Therefore, why bother to ask?

Once again, Management can improve the formal communication system and Management/Employee relations by creating a structure which responds in a timely manner. Much like the Corrective Action system, if Management consistently and speedily responds to employees' information requests, the employees will gain a higher level of trust in Management and its actions.

Not only will an improvement of the formal communication system assist the organization in its Quality initiative, it will also disarm the informal network from those who use the grapevine for more destructive uses.

After all, if Management is open with information and responsive to the employee questions and needs, what room is there for those who seek to undermine Management and the organization through rumor? Not much.

Team Deployment System

An ongoing debate exists over whether the Quality, or any, team process should be voluntary. Given that there is merit to both sides, it is left to the designers of the Quality process to determine which way will best suit the needs of their particular organization. After all, as those needs change, the Quality process will be adjusted accordingly. Of greater immediate concern is the means by which the team's success is ensured—prior to its first meeting.

Eventually, teams will form and disband at will. Groups of employees at all levels will determine needs for teams and act accordingly. Each member will have been trained in team methods and have the necessary repertoire of interpersonal and measurement tools to make the effort a success.

However, in the early days of the initiative—or even if the initiative is ongoing but has been misdirected—it is in the best interests of the organization to define the team and its purpose before the team ever meets.

Some questions which should be discussed include:

- What is the charter of the team?
    - How does its activity fit into the company's strategic goals?

- What should the team's immediate and longer-term focus be?
    - What are its objectives and priorities?

- Within what constraints and limitations will the team be working?
    - What recommendations by the team (e.g., budget, facilities, new personnel, etc.) should be included on "wish-lists" rather than as primary responses?

- What knowledge, skill, and ability are needed to address the team's focus and charter?
  - Who among the staff has that background?

- What are the expected outcomes of the team? What, if any, data requirements exist?
  - Are there time lines within which the team must work?
  - Is Management looking for the team to take action or to simply make recommendations?

- How will the team be supported?
  - What training systems exist?
  - How much time is the team given to work on its activities?
  - Will there be a liaison from Management or the Management Team to assist this team in its efforts?

These questions represent only a portion of the analysis which may be required to ensure the team's success.

Corrective Action Systems

Once a team or an individual has made a recommendation and provided adequate support, it is the responsibility of Management to respond efficiently and appropriately. Unfortunately many organizations are still floundering in this arena to the dismay of Management and employees alike.

Preferably, prior to the deployment of any teams, Management must commit to a corrective response system. This system acts as a promise of intent and made to the employees.

The systems also provides one of the greatest trust-building opportunities to be provided to Management.

Too often, the Quality Circle approach to Management response is the unwitting fall-back. The team makes its recommendations, Management thanks them politely, possibly gives them each a small gift, and sends them on their way. And that's it. Unfortunately, because so many employees have experienced this form of perceived benign neglect in past Quality initiatives as well as in day-to-day operations, Management must be all the more prepared to demonstrate a *real* difference.

As noted earlier, many organizations subscribe to what is known as the 24/72 Response System. The three-step logic of the system is as follows:

1. A team or an individual submits a recommendation to the Steering Team. The recommendation should be accompanied by data in explanation or support.

2. Within twenty-four hours, the designated Steering or Oversight Team respondent must acknowledge receipt of that recommendation. The acknowledgment can be in the form of a substantive response (i.e., direction) or simply informing the team or individual that the information was received.

3. Within seventy-two hours a substantive response is provided to the team. Substantive responses range from "Yes, go ahead" to "More Information Required" (including specific instruction regarding the information needs) to "No, with explanation."

    If the Steering Team must answer "No," they should also give direction for moving forward based on the activities, if not the results, of the team.

Not only does this system move the process forward quickly and smoothly, it provides promise and action to the employees. Management is paying attention, respects the achievements of the teams, and is supportive of their effort.

For some organizations, 72 hours is too quick a turnaround time for a substantive response at the start. No problem. Many organizations begin with what is known as a "1/5" or "1/10" Corrective Action response system. In that case, an acknowledgment is still provided within one day (i.e., the "1") but the organization allows itself either five or ten days to provide the substantive response.

Should it be necessary, an organization can begin with a "1/10," move to a "1/5," and eventually accomplish the 24/72. The best case scenario, and the most satisfying to the employees, is when the organization can and does provide immediate responses. This is the ultimate proof that the improvement initiative is constantly improving itself.

Using the Problem-Solving Process as a Management Tool

One of the most available and elegant Management tools for monitoring and overseeing team efforts is the problem-solving process.

Depending upon the structure the organization adopts, the phases range from three-step to twelve-step and everything in between. Unfortunately, organizations seem to choose their problem-solving structure more from whimsy than need.

A phased problem-solving approach provides immediate Management a structured opportunity to interact with and guide the team.

As each phase nears its end, Management should be invited to a team meeting to discuss the team's accomplishments and where they see themselves going next. This gives the manager the opportunity to intervene, if necessary, and to re-direct the team midstream—rather than risking misdirection or problems later.

Using the problem-solving structure as a Management tool makes the process more predictable and puts the managers into a less heavy-handed position than otherwise occurs.

For those organizations which are new to the idea of empowerment and self-direction, the problem-solving structure should consist of more steps. This allows managers to keep a more real-time eye on the proceedings without risking a perceived lack of trust by employees.

On the other hand, if the organization is further advanced in its development toward an empowered work force, fewer steps are required. Management trusts that the team will move forward appropriately and with little intervention or direction needed.

For those organizations which start out with Management visiting the teams at the conclusion of each phase, one of the ways by which they demonstrate their trust is by reducing their participation. Specific phases are identified for Management invitation. Otherwise, the team is left to invite their manager as the need arises. The trick, if there is one, is to pay attention and apply lessons learned.

More improvement efforts have "failed" from lack of attention than from any other malady.

Luckily, the disease is not terminal. In fact, for those organizations which have found themselves turning around what were thought to be failed efforts, the results have far exceeded anything managers or employees had ever expected.

PART 4

Some
Final Words

CHAPTER 10

On Empowerment

Probably one of the least understood concepts in Quality is that of empowerment.

Those who want it don't have it. Those who have it don't want to give it up.

And no one quite knows what to do about it. The problem is, empowerment has some of the strongest potential impact in the overall process. Empowerment, like everything else in Quality, is a process—and it is a challenging one.

Empowerment, simply defined, is the process of moving responsibility and authority downward into the organization in such a way that those who have the most and best information and expertise about a process are the ones who make the decisions which affect it.

Empowerment, as a process, is progressive. It requires analysis and understanding of the goals and strategy of the organization, in concert with the knowledge, expertise, abilities, and needs of managers and employees.

In this chapter, empowerment will be presented from a number of different perspectives. They include the:

- Objectives of Empowerment
- Misconceptions about Empowerment
- Process of Empowerment.

Objectives of Empowerment

The primary objective of empowering personnel is to promote continuous improvement activities by:

- Moving the decision-making process to the lowest realistic level of the organization

- Providing Management with time to strategize and implement improvements to their own processes

- Restoring pride and dignity throughout the organization.

Please note that the primary objective is to use empowerment as a tool towards continuous improvement.

Empowerment tends to be looked at as an end in and of itself. It is not. It is part of the overall continuous improvement process. In fact, empowerment should be viewed as one of the arsenal of tools available to Management to ensure the success of the Quality effort.

Moving the Decision-Making Process to the Lowest Realistic Level of the Organization

You will note the language used in this objective: the decision-making process is moved to the lowest *realistic* level of the organization. As part of the empowerment process, that level moves progressively downward through the ranks of the organization.

It is unrealistic and unfair to dump decision-making responsibility onto people who have neither the skills nor the information to take on that responsibility. But it is also unrealistic and unfair to withhold the decision-making responsibility from people who do have the ability and the information to make those decisions.

In most organizations, decisions are made at a much higher level than they should be. There are a number of reasons why.

In some organizations, there is a general fear among middle and lower level managers of what would happen if they moved ahead without prior consent from Senior Management. When that is the case the environment in the organization is one which does not support risk-taking. That should be a first concern in the Quality process.

Because empowerment is a process, it must be implemented progressively as the managers and employees at each level gain the knowledge and ability needed to take on the new responsibilities.

Part of that progression must be a focus on data. No manager or employee should be asked or able to make decisions about a process unless there are timely, high integrity data systems in place. The progressive approach also alleviates the concerns of many Middle Managers who see themselves as potentially being made obsolete.

It is the responsibility of Senior Management to ensure that the appropriate knowledge and skills are made available to those people in the organization who should be making decisions.

As Management moves through the assessment and planning process, they will glean a great deal of information which will assist them in best strategizing the empowerment process.

Providing Management with Time to Strategize and Implement Improvements to their Own Processes

We tend to forget that Management has processes which they own. In fact, usually managers tend to forget that fact as well. No surprise, actually. Most managers—at all levels—spend so much time dealing with work that takes place many levels below them that they have little to no time left to focus on the processes which most directly affect them.

The really unfortunate aspect of the current situation is that managers are usually making decisions about which they have, at best, a limited understanding. And they are expected to make learned decisions about those processes. This results in both wasted time and effort.

Instead, as managers move the responsibility and authority to people who do have the knowledge, expertise, and data about the process to be improved, they become free to focus on the processes within which they work.

Managers must be given the time to examine their own responsibilities to determine which processes, or parts of processes, are owned by them. Once those have been determined, managers must next identify ways by which those processes can be improved.

Restoring Pride and Dignity Throughout the Organization

Empowerment, as it is integrated into the Quality process, is a visible, tangible demonstration of interest and trust in all levels of employees from the Management group. By moving responsibility and authority down into the organization, managers and employees are, in effect, told that they are trusted, will not be punished and, in fact, will be rewarded for their efforts.

We have become used to complaining about work situations with little to no hope of change. The empowerment process, as part of the Quality effort, starts by giving us hope. From there we move to taking on responsibilities which should rightfully be ours.

Each of us is an expert at the process within which we work. We have the knowledge and experience to understand what works and what doesn't. Couple that with data to support our observations and the responsibility and authority to do something about it and, suddenly, work is a great place to be.

Several Misconceptions about Empowerment

The first misconception is that either you are empowered or you aren't. In fact, the levels of empowerment are developmental. These levels are achieved as the organization grows in its overall Quality process and as the managers and employees learn more about their responsibilities in this regard.

As a result, it is unrealistic to believe that if you are to be empowered, then, from the first, you must be fully empowered. Nothing less will do.

This is an expectation often encountered as organizations are working on the empowerment process. If empowerment is treated developmentally, and that is made clear to everyone from the first, then there are fewer unrealistic expectations. There is also more interest across the organization in finding out how to expand the boundaries of empowerment.

The second misconception is that empowerment only applies to line employees. Not true. The fact is, empowerment applies throughout the organization. Executive Management must learn to empower their direct reports. And for each subsequent level the same applies. Just as no one is exempt from Quality, a part of that process is that no one is excluded from being empowered.

After all, it is in the best interests of the organization and all who work there that *each person* be empowered. That means that those who have the knowledge and the expertise to make the best possible decisions are the ones making them.

As long as each person knows and understands the goals and strategy of the organization and risk is controlled by working within the PDSA, there is no loss attached to empowerment.

The third misconception is that empowerment creates anarchy. This is not true if Management does its job. If empowerment is treated as a process and the implementation of the process is progressive, there can be no anarchy.

Each level of the organization will require training in skills such as measurement, decision-making, problem-solving, and in many cases, critical thinking, before any person—manager or employee—can be fully empowered to take on strategic as well as tactical responsibility. But in the meantime, each person is involved in a developmental process which nets positive results both for the individual and for the organization.

The last misconception included here is that Management becomes impotent as a result of empowerment. This is the biggest fear and obstacle facing the empowerment process.

Given that empowerment is progressive, Management remains actively involved in all aspects of its implementation over the course of time. As the need for training is identified, Management must work to strategize how best to utilize that training. As data systems are designed and implemented, Management must be involved in the system development and subsequent corrective actions resulting from the data.

Management must, at all times, be the provider of the "what" and "why" components of the question. Managers explain to their improvement teams *what* they are to focus on and *why* that focus is important to the team and to the organization. These focus areas come from the overall strategy and specific strategic focus areas developed by the Management group.

Teams are then empowered, using the PDSA structure, to identify innovative ways of *how* to address those focus areas.

As a result of the assessment phase, Management will be directing the activities of the teams. Managers will be actively clearing away obstacles from the path of the teams. They will also be identifying obstacles which the teams could not be expected to know about. And managers will also be busy coordinating with other managers to ensure cooperation and integration throughout the team effort.

It has most often been the case that the exclusive focus of empowerment efforts has been at the line level. This has put unrealistic expectations onto the lowest levels, while at the same time, ignoring the managers' needs for empowerment.

In order to fully benefit from the expertise in the organization, everyone must be allowed to learn and grow by being given responsibility and authority to make things better.

Process of Empowerment

This is going to sound familiar. If empowerment is a process, and that process is one which needs to be improved, then the place to start is with the PDSA structure. By using the PDSA you will be able to develop a strategic empowerment plan with reduced risk to the organization. The structure will also limit the perceived threat to those managers who would be inclined to react in that way.

Begin by assessing what, strategically, must be addressed first.

What are the empowerment needs of the organization? Do they reside at the middle level of Management? On the front line? Among a particular employee group?

In what ways should the empowerment process be manifest in order to have the greatest positive impact on the organization?

Are there data systems in place to support the development of the empowerment process?

What are the training and personal developmental needs of the managers and employees who will be involved in the pilot? By combining data acquired during the Assessment phase with specific data gathering related to the empowerment process, Management will be able to strategize and optimize the empowerment process from the first. From that point forward, managers can begin, with the assistance of employees, to implement that process.

The reaction of employees at the lower levels of the organization will be most noticeable first. Those employees, who have often had the most to complain about with the least recourse, are usually so pleased with the empowerment process that it becomes a catalyst to even greater improvement efforts.

The reaction of Middle Management will have to be monitored. Remember, this group of people also lived through the misadventures of the previous implementation efforts. Many have left or lost jobs because of cost-cutting efforts which were erroneously tied to "Quality programs." As a result, Senior Management must work to reassure and support Middle Managers as they learn their part of the Quality and empowerment processes. At no time should any employee at any level be concerned that, as a result of the Quality process, his job is in jeopardy.

It must constantly be remembered that empowerment is a cooperative system based on open communication and reciprocity. Managers and employees must work together to identify workable initial boundaries of empowerment which satisfy both the employees' need to stretch and Management's need to control risk. From there, Management and employees work to develop means of widening those boundaries as a result of increased learning, ability, and trust.

In fact, in a truly empowered organization, employees take on the role of teachers to Management. How else can managers know how to direct their immediate organizational improvement efforts if not by hearing from their customers—the employees?

Conversely, what better way is there to expand the knowledge of your employees than by working with them to understand the goals and strategy of the organization?

This type of reciprocity leads to mutual empowerment and satisfaction throughout the organization.

CHAPTER 11

Taking the Pain out of Quality Implementation

No matter how well you plan and execute the Quality implementation process, some obstacles will be encountered. Unfortunately, many individuals and organizations upon encountering obstacles assume the effort is not working and either stop or slow down.

Not necessary. In fact, the obstacles can and should be diagnosed during the Assessment and Planning phase. How to address those obstacles should then be included in the strategy and implementation structure.

By being proactive, you will be able to reduce the impact of some obstacles and avoid others altogether.

But, what are the common obstacles? Some of them have already been discussed in previous chapters. Others have been alluded to but not addressed directly. And, as always, there are more than are presented here. Those will be apparent to you in analyzing your own organization.

The purpose of this chapter is to provide an overview of some of the common obstacles encountered during the implementation process, an understanding of why those obstacles exist, and some strategies by which to address the common obstacles and avoid others.

The Obstacles and Their Root Causes

Management "Alleged" Support

There is a common misconception that Senior Management has little to no intention of implementing the Quality process themselves. It is thought that Quality is another program which has been delegated to the masses—until Management comes up with another idea.

This perception exists because employees rarely see the efforts and struggles of Senior Management as they learn and work the implementation process themselves.

An easy way to build trust in the organization, and support for the Quality effort, is for Senior Management to make their implementation process visible to the employees.

This does not mean that managers must share all information about their process. Some information—no matter at what level the team resides—must remain confidential in order to develop team support.

Instead, it means that Senior Management must communicate what it is that they are doing to drive and support the Quality approach.

Be visible. Talk to employees, knowledgeably, about process improvement. Don't be a spokesperson of slogans and hyperbole. Instead, demonstrate an active interest in the challenges and successes of all employees as the organization goes through this transformation. In effect, don't let the question of the extent of your support arise.

And if, for some reason, Senior Management believes that they are exempt from the process, they will soon find out that they are wrong.

As customers it is incumbent upon the employees of the organization—at all levels—to explain to Management why it is important for them to participate in the Quality process. Unless they are so informed, and are provided with data to support those allegations, Senior Management has no way of knowing the effect their ignorance of the process is having on the organization.

The Middle Management Balk

Of all the groups affected by Quality, the Middle Managers perceive themselves as having the most to lose. From their perspective, if the implementation effort succeeds, they have worked themselves out of a job. Again, this is not an unfair nor unfounded school of thought. What with historical cost-cutting through supposed Quality initiatives, and the perceived easiest way to cut costs being lay-offs and flattening the organization, Middle Managers have had a right to be concerned.

Senior Management must work with all levels of Management and Supervision to create and maintain an environment supportive of the organization's goals with improvement and innovation as the norms. This means focusing managers not on the daily processes of their workers, but on improvement processes which will help the organization achieve its strategic direction and intent.

If Senior Management truly understands the concept of building systems of cooperation, they will know that those systems will be greatly inhibited—and possibly fail—without the knowledge and expertise of those in the middle ranks who know how to make the overall organizational system work.

Middle Management must be treated as a resource to the organization. They are an asset which can facilitate successful Quality implementation faster than anyone expected.

The "This Too Shall Pass" — "Not This Again" Syndrome

Many employees, especially those who have been in the organization a long time, will take a wait-and-see attitude toward the Quality effort. Not surprising when viewed from their perspective. They have seen it all before. They have also learned that if they sit back and wait long enough, this "program" will go away just like all the rest.

By building buy-in at all levels of Management from the first, and working through the Assessment and Planning phase, employees are presented with what looks like, and is, a business strategy—not another program.

Historically, many implementation efforts have been sabotaged because the lower levels of the organization—both Supervision/Management and employees—were left out of the understanding process. Instead, they were left to perform the necessary actions of the Quality effort as well as those for which they were already responsible.

Being proactive in bringing Middle and Lower Management into the process goes a long way toward alleviating this obstacle.

And for those employees who are absolutely resistant to the Quality process, it may be necessary to work with them on a one-on-one basis to assure them of the organization's commitment to Quality, the importance of their participation, and to strategize ways by which they can be brought actively into the implementation process.

The Worker Revolt

This obstacle is the manifestation of empowerment gone awry. Unless empowerment is strategized and implemented as a developmental process rooted in continuous improvement, there is a risk of creating anarchy.

Employees must be aware of the initial boundaries and strategies of empowerment. It may be something as simple as giving a team free rein to make decisions with the understanding that they will not be able to ask, for example, for new employees or capital equipment. The reason for those boundaries must also be explained to the employees.

Remember, in a Quality environment, there is no such thing as a manager telling a team "no" without accompanying the response with information and data. It is then up to the team to either find another way to address the issue, identify additional indicators which would provide the manager with reason to adopt the corrective action, or determine a phased approach which would not be in violation of the organization's strategy.

By explaining from the start what the empowerment process is and how it will progress, neither managers nor employees have unrealistic expectations. Misunderstandings common to the empowerment process are avoided. And as the empowerment process expands so do the boundaries, giving employees the responsibility and authority to make decisions with more widespread impact in the organization.

Analysis Paralysis

This obstacle often extends throughout the organization. There is sometimes a tendency among teams to be hesitant about taking action. Lack of data becomes an excuse rather than a driver. This occurs for a variety of reasons.

In some cases, there really aren't adequate data from which to make a knowledgeable decision. If that is the problem, indicators and measurement systems which will help to provide the necessary information must be developed.

In other cases, when it is a case of Analysis Paralysis, people fear taking risks. If that is the case, Management must identify the source of that fear and take action toward its removal. Unless every employee believes that he can only be rewarded for his improvement efforts—and that he is not risking the wrath of any supervisor or manager—the Quality effort will become stalled and possibly die.

Some Strategies for Success

Get Educated

Begin your Quality quest by having all Management personnel start an education process together. Access books, videos, and articles. Find out about and attend seminars. Then take that information and, as a Management team, apply the theory to determine how it fits—or doesn't fit—your organization.

Make a commitment to learning and education from the first. And then extend that commitment so that it is apparent and available to everyone throughout the organization.

Treat Quality as a Way of Doing Business

Don't fall into the trap of fancy announcements and big promises. As you enter into the Quality process, you will find that there is a strength and dignity to the process which doesn't allow for bells and whistles.

There is a tendency to want to assure everyone that this time it will be different. Instead of doing that, *show* them. From the Management perspective, work the assessment and planning of the effort so that it can be smoothly integrated as a part of daily operations—not something superimposed upon the "real work" to be done.

From the employee perspective, keep an open mind and work with the process as a means of achieving your goals.

Be Strategic

Get into the habit of thinking strategically about anything you are about to do. Look at your actions from the perspective of your internal and external customers and suppliers as well as from your immediate process perspective.

Think about cooperation and coordination of actions across the organization, and analyze any actions or proposals for actions from the perspective of the overall organizational goals and strategy.

Use the "If/Then" strategy. When determining an action or direction, first ask yourself, "If we do this, then the outcome will be . . . . However, if we do *this,* then the outcome will be . . . ."

By going through the "If/Then" steps, all contingencies can be identified, their potential outcomes predicted, and the most appropriate next step determined. Using this strategy also keeps individuals and teams from jumping to conclusions and not-well-thought out actions before they adversely affect the organization.

Design the Implementation Effort as a Parallel Path

One of the ways to avoid the "Analysis Paralysis" obstacle from the first is to view the implementation process as a parallel path. Senior Management should not wait until it has gained all the knowledge possible about Quality before beginning the implementation effort. If they wait that long, chances are the competition will have already passed the organization by.

Instead, Management must understand that it has made a commitment to continuous learning as part of the Quality effort. As such, there is no end to the knowledge that they can and must attain to successfully drive the effort. As a result, it is possible to complete the Assessment and Planning Phase, begin the implementation process, and continue to pursue more knowledge concurrently with implementation.

This results in adequate information from which to design the implementation effort, activity toward the ongoing success and improvement of the organization, and an increased ability to analyze the results and ramifications of the effort as Management's learning increases.

Use the Teach/Do Philosophy

This may be one of the single most powerful strategies in Quality implementation. Too many organizations have hindered the implementation process, both in terms of time and money, by providing extensive up-front training with little or no implementation structure attached.

Instead, as the implementation process progresses, training should be provided only when necessary and only on those skills and tools which will be immediately implemented.

As part of, and in response to, the overall strategy, a strategic and tactical training plan should be devised. Incorporating the Teach/Do philosophy into the implementation process alleviates concerns among both managers and employees about leveraging training time with operations time. Costs are contained and results are immediate.

CHAPTER 12

Roles and Responsibilities

Given the changes in the operation of the organization, we must be prepared to take a look at the changes in our individual roles and responsibilities.

Quality redefines the organization and everyone in it. There is a shared, understood purpose. There is a strategy to support that purpose. And there are implementation activities to realize the aims set for the organization. None of this can happen if the individuals do not understand and accept the changes necessary in their own activities.

You will recall that two of the principles of Quality are to reduce waste and to build on the best. Those concepts have direct applicability to the analysis and implementation of the new roles and responsibilities.

Each employee and manager, in teams and as individuals, should take the time to analyze the new responsibilities he has taken in the organization. What are the new requirements? What activities are attached to those requirements? What assistance will he need in being able to accomplish his new role?

From there, implementation of the improvements is a process in which, as individuals and teams, each employee studies his "old way" of doing things, specifically with an eye towards building blocks for success (build on the best) and improvement opportunities (reducing waste).

As always, implementation of the new roles and responsibilities is realized through the structure and use of the PDSA cycle.

Another principle, and one which has an interesting twist to it in this context, is to focus on the customer. When looking at the organization from an internal, hierarchical perspective, who is the customer? Anyone at a lower organizational level than you. For Executive Management, everyone in the organization—from your direct reports to front line people you may never see—are your customers. For anyone in a Management position, those who report to you are your customers.

Once again, we are faced with the analysis of what our customers need. How can we create total customer satisfaction unless we know what the customers are looking for?

As a supplier, every manager must make the effort to find out what his customer's requirements are and how best to fulfill them.

From the customer (direct report) perspective, there is a responsibility to ensure that your supplier (manager) understands your needs. This will entail open and honest communication with a real desire to improve the overall process.

In effect, every employee at every level, is responsible for "training" his direct manager. Each employee, has to approach the Quality process as one which will involve direct communication with a focus on cooperation, coordination, and building systems for improvement.

Remember, this is all within the context of the overall organizational goals and strategies. You are all working toward the same end.

From the Management Perspective

For Management, implementation of the Quality process means that you have a new focus. You are now able to access expertise from within your organization, receive new data which are more timely and realistic, and make better informed decisions.

There is a shared purpose in the work you do. Rather than having an adversarial or near-adversarial relationship with your employees, you have the opportunity to share the burden of the improvement process with people who want to see it succeed as much as, if not more than, you do.

And, finally, instead of simply being managers of people, you have the opportunity to utilize your personal expertise to make your own contributions to the organization. Providing your expertise, particularly to those to whom you report, and serving as part of the Management team, you are able to affect sorely-needed improvements to the systems.

You are also given the opportunity to look to the future. Rather than focusing all your time and energy on the day-to-day immediate activities, you have the opportunity to be a thinker and a visionary. You will have a view of the capabilities and potential for the products and services of your organization that few will share.

It will be your responsibility to share that information and build upon it to keep the organization viable, increase its share of the market, and delight your customers, both internal and external, with the improvements you generate.

From the Employee Perspective

For the employee, Quality means that you will have the opportunity and the responsibility to share your knowledge of the current operation of the processes within which you work. You will be able to change those aspects of the process which need to be changed and share your knowledge with other employees.

Instead of your successes and improvements being informally communicated to a limited audience, you will have the opportunity to actively help others build on your improvements, making them applicable to other parts of the process. You will also have the opportunity to build on your own accomplishments. By working in a dedicated team effort, with everyone involved and with Management working to clear obstacles out of your way, you will be able to continuously improve your process.

Management's primary focus in support of your activities will be to assist you in finding ways to learn and grow both personally and professionally. As you focus more on the needs of the process in concert with the needs of the business, you will gain insight and experience. No matter at what level of the organization you function, your business acumen will be accessed and utilized to benefit not only you, personally, but the organization as a whole.

You will have pride in your work and in yourself. The Quality effort, supported by managers and employees at all levels, will allow you the opportunity to become a valued thinking entity inside the organization.

Each person will know that his or her contributions to the organization are absolutely necessary to ensure the ongoing success, let alone existence, of the organization.

And for the Senior Executives

In your case, you have the absolute, incomparable joy of being able to dream about what the organization could be, to communicate that vision to the rest of the organization, and to see your dream realized.

Is there anything better?

Quality as Strategy

There has been a grave misunderstanding in industry regarding the role and definition of Quality. Because of all of the attention placed on Quality during the last twenty years, there has been a tendency to pigeonhole the field and its application as if it is something separate and apart from the real workings of organizations. As if it can be superficially applied, somehow, to the products and services produced.

This does both the field and industry a grave disservice. Quality is neither superficial nor something which is externally applied. It is a strategy and tactic which must be planned and built in from the first as well as integrated throughout the life of the product or service.

Quality is the way that organizations strategically differentiate themselves from their competition. This means that Quality belongs to Management, because strategy belongs to Management.

Quality and Strategy

As part of the strategic planning process, Management goes through a definitional process. In that process, members of Management decide how they must define the organization and its direction to ensure its success. Whether the timeframe for success and direction is measured in years or decades doesn't matter. Neither does it matter whether the organization measures its success based on shareholder value, profits, or marketshare. What does matter is that the organization knows what it must do and where it is going as a result of that Management definition.

As a strategy, Quality is a simple and elegant approach to the way the organization operates. It is based on the premise that the organization, as defined by its strategy, is to work in a particular direction toward a defined set of goals. These goals are in the best interests of the organization, its shareholders, and its stakeholders in the form of management, employees, customers, and suppliers.

The organization must use the most straightforward and direct means of achieving those goals. Unnecessary complexity leading to unnecessary costs must be eliminated.

In place of that complexity there should be a clear and direct approach to all activities related to the organization. Everyone must work towards those goals, in concert, to ensure that every aspect of the organization is designed to succeed.

Quality, Competition, and Customer Expectations

Quality as a strategic differentiator also applies to the ways by which the organization addresses its competition. Organizations must take advantage of the learning opportunities availed them by their competitors.

Industry knowledge is easily gained. Trend data and market information are readily available. The means by which the competition operates, both internally and with their customers, is usually apparent if one knows what one is looking for.

Each organization must actively study its competitors in order to determine what customers have been taught to expect. Customers do not view their supplying organizations in a vacuum. Therefore, the supplying organizations must view themselves in the same context in which they are placed by their customers.

Further, because customers do not work exclusively with one organization or one industry, each organization must expand its thinking to include other "buying opportunities" which the customer experiences. This is particularly the case when service is a comparative and strategic differentiator.

Customers, even when not dealing in a retail environment, bring their retail experiences and expectations with them. From the customer's perspective, good service and high levels of customer attention are a must. Telephone servers and call systems are compared across industries—not simply on a basis of how you or your organization presents yours. How long your customers wait and how easy it is to reach a person become competitive differentiators.

Customer expectations are no longer defined on a by-industry basis. They are defined on a by-experience basis. And that experience expands from your organization to include all other organizations with which the customer does business—personally and professionally.

The stakes are high. They are also manageable. With adequate attention and efficient information sharing systems among and between individuals, departments, and divisions, the necessary knowledge is readily available for use and sharing.

What It Takes

All that is necessary for success is to ensure that Quality is incorporated into operations as a strategy and as an expectation. The rest will fall into place.

Senior Management must take the time, by far the most valuable and least available commodity, to determine what needs to be done. The outcomes of those decisions must be communicated to and understood by all Management across the organization. Systematic methods of further communicating and managing to those needs must be established. Participation at all levels must be designed and ensured.

If everybody knows where they are going and why, they will do all that they can to help get there. It is in their best interests to do so. It is the ultimate win-win.

About the Author

Leslie L. Kossoff, founder and principal of Kossoff Management Consulting, is the leading expert in quality and productivity improvement for a broad range of industries and clients in the United States and Europe. She has been designing and implementing Quality systems for more than 20 years, assisting such prominent clients as Kraft Foods, 3M, and TRW. She also actively focuses her attention on the unique needs of small- and medium-sized firms in achieving their continuous improvement goals.

Kossoff enjoys an outstanding reputation as an invited speaker at professional and educational conferences throughout the United States. During her long-term alliance with Dr. W. Edwards Deming, founder of the Quality Movement and the "Japanese Industrial Miracle," she also assisted in his client consultations and his seminars speaking and consulting specifically on implementation obstacles and strategies. Deming declared Kossoff, "Quite simply, one of the *best* at implementation."

Kossoff has published numerous articles pertaining to managing and implementing quality and productivity improvement initiatives. She is the author of the book *Managing for Quality: How to Implement and Manage a Business Strategy of Continuous Improvement.* Her forthcoming books include *Executive Thinking* and the *Managing for Quality Field Guide.*

Kossoff is included in the *Who's Who Registry of Global Business Leaders* and has been a member of the Judges Panel for the Sterling Award of Orange County. She holds a Bachelor and a Master of Arts degree from San Francisco State University and a Master of Science from the University of Oregon.